News Anchors of CBS 19

DEVELOPMENT OF FACIAL TRAITS

Make a difference in Racial Problem.

This book helps connect people in the world.

You can help to make it happen.

8-18-2017

DEVELOPMENT OF
FACIAL TRAITS

CONNECTING PEOPLE IN THE WORLD

KAM CHIANG

DEVELOPMENT OF FACIAL TRAITS
Available from Amazon.com and other retailers.
E-book is available on Kindle.
Visit www.FacialTraits.com.

WE ALL CAME FROM THE SAME ANCESTORS.

Why do people look different on different continents?

In this book,
you will learn how and why early humans developed different
facial characteristics
in different regions of the world before they became
genetic traits.

CONTENTS

PREFACE

Do you know why many Caucasian people have blue and green eyes, thin lips, and high and narrow noses? Why do African people have low and wide noses with full lips? Why do many Asian people have slender eyes with short eyelashes? These questions seem to be very simple but are hard to answer. Of course, they are all genetic. These facial traits have been passed down for generations. What we don't know is how these facial characteristics developed before they became genetic. Why do people from one continent look alike yet look so different from people of other continents? As of today, anthropologists and scientists still can't explain the development of each facial trait and its origin.

Whether you are an evolutionist who believes that all human beings belong to one single species, *Homo sapiens*, or a religious person who believes we are all descendants of Adam and Eve, you still have to explain why human beings from different continents look different. People of each continent have developed their own distinct facial and physical characteristics. As a result, early anthropologists have classified people into several major races and many subraces. Often, different scientists have different opinions, thus leading to different classifications. Modern studies have indicated that race is not biological. In recent decades, the use of the term *race* has been strongly opposed by the United Nations and many other organizations. In this book, I use the geographic name for people who share similar facial and physical characteristics with others in the same geographic area, using the word *race* only when needed.

Anthropologists have long believed that the development of races has a lot to do with climate. However, they have not explained exactly how the climate has caused different facial characteristics other than skin and hair color. Normally, paleontologists rely on fossils and surrounding rocks to reconstruct the organisms and interpret the past environment. To study the facial traits of early humans is extremely difficult. In addition, there are no photos, drawings, or written records of what we looked like in the past, and there are hardly any fossil remains. Our facial traits are made of flesh, soft tissues, and cartilage, all of which decay soon after we die and seldom are preserved. A few scattered skulls and skeletons of early human beings give us only some idea of what their bodies and heads looked like and very little insight into their facial characteristics or how they developed. Scientists seldom talk about this subject, mainly because they know very little about it. Until now, the development of our facial traits has remained a big mystery.

For the first time, this book opens the door of this mystery. It takes you back in time tens or hundreds of thousands of years ago. You will understand where your ancestors came from: their livelihoods, habitats, climates, and environments. Together with the influence of regional civilization and culture, early humans have developed different facial characteristics in different regions of the world. Over time, their new facial characteristics became genetic among people in the same region. Today, their descendants inherit similar traits from their ancestors, even though they are no longer living in the same environment and place. Each trait tells a story of our ancestors. Together, they form the history of early humans.

I use what we know today to predict what might have happened in the past. The present is a key to the past. When you use the right key, you can unlock any mystery. You will find that my theories and interpretations solve every mystery. They are interesting and fascinating yet believable. Nothing in this book is too scientific that the public may not understand, and it does not contain controversial arguments that contradict the facts. Everything in this book is common knowledge and our daily life, which I have applied appropriately to interpret the development of our facial traits. I also use examples and analogies to aid your understanding.

The contents of this book are my own personal opinions and logical interpretations realized without the support of fossil remains. They are new theories, which have not been proven right or wrong. The reader's discretion is advised.

CHAPTER 1

INTRODUCTION

Scientists believe that our planet earth is about 4.6 billion years old. The earliest plant fossils found were algae, which date to one billion years ago. The earliest invertebrates commonly found on earth were trilobites, which date to about five hundred million years ago. They look like today's "rolly pollies" with bigger body and longer legs on both sides. Since then, many species of organisms have been found on earth. Some were short-lived, lasting only for a few million years. Others continued for hundreds of millions of years. Fossils of fish, such as sharks, were found as far back as four hundred million years ago. Dinosaurs came to dominate the world 65 to 225 million years ago.

It is believed that our human ancestors appeared on earth two million years ago, based on paleontological and archaeological studies. Since there is not enough evidence to provide a complete interpretation of human evolution, origin, and migration, there are many theories, hypotheses, speculations, and religious beliefs. Often, theories and interpretations change as new evidence is discovered. In this book, I am not going to discuss the origin of human beings and whether we evolved from primates or are descendants of Adam and Eve. I will leave this subject for readers to decide.

Instead, I will concentrate on what has happened to human faces and bodies since emerging in this world.

It is an undeniable fact that people look different in different regions of the world. In each continent, people have their own unique characteristics that distinguish them from people of other continents. In earlier days, anthropologists and scientists have used these facial traits and body characteristics to divide people into different races and subraces. They believed there was biological separation among people, which led to a hypothesis that we descended from different human lineages.

Previously, the earliest fossils of modern human beings were found at Kibish near the Omo River in southwestern Ethiopia, eastern Africa, which date to 195,000 years old. Consequently, a recent theory suggests that early humans emerged in Ethiopia. Before the end of the Ice Age (about ten thousand years ago), they had spread to all continents in the world, except for Antarctica. Archaeological findings and dating indicate they had lived in Africa for tens of thousands of years, mostly along the Nile River and on the northern coast of Africa and in southern Africa. Their earliest migration out of Africa and into the Arabian Peninsula was dated 125,000 years ago. The great migration of early humans from Africa to Asia began about seventy thousand years ago. From Southeast Asia, some of them crossed over to New Guinea and Australia, and others went north to China, then to North America and South America. Migration into Europe occurred later, about forty-five thousand years ago. (Note: the above information and data are obtained from Wikipedia and other Internet sources. Recent publications state that the human remains found at Jebel Irhoud, Morocco, western Africa, were about 300,000 years old. This new discovery suggests that our ancestors emerged earlier than we previously thought.)

Assume the theory that the earliest human beings first appeared in Africa is correct and that they migrated and spread to different continents in the world. It suggests that all people in the world came from the same group of ancestors. Theoretically, we should all have the same appearance as the African people or whatever the early humans looked like in Africa. Why do people look different in different regions in the world today?

In the following chapters, you will soon learn my theories and interpretations of how the climate, environment, culture, and way of life have caused changes in facial and body characteristics of early humans in different regions in the world.

CHAPTER 2

DEVELOPMENT OF FACIAL TRAITS AMONG EUROPEAN, ASIAN, AND AFRICAN PEOPLE

After early human beings emerged in Africa, they migrated to and settled in three large continents: Africa, Asia, and Europe. In each of these three continents, their populations grew, and they spread to cover almost every habitable area. After tens of thousands of years, their facial and body characteristics also gradually changed. People of each continent developed new facial and physical traits, which are different from the people of other continents. In this chapter, you will learn what has caused the change in facial features of each group and how they developed new characteristics.

Since people of the same continent have similar facial traits and body characteristics, it is easy to group them as one. There are many ethnic groups in each continent. Many of them are divided because of different geographic locations, languages, cultures, and customs. They will not be described separately in this book because they still share similar traits within their groups. The three large groups of people are European, Asian, and African. Their populations have now reached almost six billion people.

DEFINITION OF GEOGRAPHIC GROUPS OF PEOPLE:
European people in this book refer to all people whose ancestors were indigenous to the continent of Europe. This includes people of all countries in Europe as well as Europeans who migrated to other continents, such as North America, Central and South America, Australia, and Africa. They are commonly called Caucasian or white people. Note: European people in this chapter do not include Middle Eastern and Indian people, who will be described in chapter 3.

Asian people in this book refer to all people whose ancestors were indigenous to Asia and Southeast Asia. This includes people of all countries in Asia—namely, China, Korea, Japan, and Mongolia, and in Southeast Asia—namely, Vietnam, Laos, Myanmar, Bhutan, Thailand, Cambodia, Malaysia, Brunei, Philippines, Singapore, and Indonesia. They are commonly called Asian people. Note: this discussion does not include people living in countries west of China and Myanmar.

African people in this book refer to all people whose ancestors were indigenous to Africa. It also includes Africans who migrated to other continents. They are also called black people. Note: this discussion does not include some people in northern Africa, who are grouped with Middle Eastern people.

GEOGRAPHIC LOCATION OF EACH CONTINENT AND CLIMATE: The continent of Europe is bordered by the Atlantic Ocean in the west, the Mediterranean Sea in the south, and the Arctic Ocean in the north. In the east, Europe is connected to the continent of Asia. Together, this landmass is called Eurasia.

Most of Europe is situated north of 40° latitude. The northern portion of Europe extends into the Arctic Circle. Early humans settled in Europe during the Ice Age. Note: there were several ice ages recorded in the geological history of earth. The last Ice Age began two million years ago. It consisted of four glacial periods of very cold climates separated by interglacial periods of warmer temperatures (Carl O. Dunbar and Karl M. Waage, *Historical Geology*, 1969). It is also known as the recent Ice Age, which ended about ten thousand to eleven thousand years ago. In this book, I will use ten thousand years ago for simplicity. The temperature was much colder than now. During the peak of the Ice Age, ice sheets covered the entire northern Europe, including Great Britain and Germany. Great Britain was connected to the continent of Europe due to lower sea levels (most of the precipitation had formed into ice and snow on land without returning to the ocean). The temperatures we experience today are much warmer than ten thousand years ago because we are now living in the postglacial period and experiencing global warming.

The continent of Asia is the eastern landmass of Eurasia. It is situated on both sides of the Tropic of Cancer. Most of the area is south of 45° latitude, except for Siberia, where there are very few inhabitants. It extends far south to the equator. It is bordered in the east by the Pacific Ocean and in the southwest by the Indian Ocean. The climate is mild and warm with four distinct seasons. Rainfalls are frequent and abundant locally. There are no large deserts, except for the extreme west of China and Mongolia. The landmass is broken up into many islands in Southeast Asia, where the climate is hot and humid, primarily tropical and equatorial weather. Generally speaking, Asia is a warm continent.

The continent of Africa is located south of Europe, separated by the Mediterranean Sea. It is bordered in the west by the Atlantic Ocean and in the east by the Indian Ocean. It lies on both sides of the equator. The northern portion of the continent is mostly occupied by the Sahara Desert, which is the largest desert in the world. Africa is the hottest among the three continents.

SCOPE OF DESCRIPTION: Each facial trait described in this book is a common characteristic of a geographic group of people. It does not mean that all people of that group must have the same feature. Some people of another continent may also have the same characteristic. Immigrants from another continent may bear the facial traits of their original geographic area. Many people do not know that they have ancestors from another region. For example, some Caucasian people are part Mongolian—people who came to Europe seven hundred years ago when Genghis Khan conquered the west—and they may bear some features of Asian people. Furthermore, we are now living in a world of globalization. It is common to find different groups of people living on the same continent. Children of mixed marriages bear mixed facial characteristics. Often, it is hard to determine which group of people they truly belong to. As you read this book, please remember that my descriptions and interpretations apply only to people whose ancestors were truly indigenous to the named geographic continent and that there are variations of traits within each group of people.

In the following sections, each of our facial and bodily traits is described separately. I offer my theories and interpretations and explain how and why these traits were developed among each group of people. Of course, many of our facial traits are genetic and hereditary. What you will learn is how our facial characteristics developed before they became genetic. (For your personal interest, after you read the FACTS AND QUESTIONS in each section, try to answer some of the questions yourself before reading THEORIES AND INTERPRETATIONS. You may want to ask your friends or family the same questions and see if they give different answers.)

2.1

NOSES

FACTS AND QUESTIONS: The nose sits in the middle of the face, and it has distinct characteristics that distinguish people from different continents. European people have high and narrow noses. African people have low and wide or flat noses. Asian people have medium-size noses, which are not as high and narrow as the Europeans and not as low and wide as the Africans. Why do Europeans have high and narrow noses? Some of them even have arched noses, which are rare among Africans and Asians. How did African people develop low and wide noses?

If you observe carefully, then you will also notice that Europeans' noses are lean, with very little fatty tissues. Their nose tips are pointed, usually pointing downward. Why did European people have lean noses with pointed tips? Africans' nose tips are exactly opposite. Their nose tips are round with more fatty tissues, facing front or slightly up. Why did African people have fleshy, round nose tips? Asians' nose tips bear the intermediate characteristics between the two, neither as lean and pointed as the Europeans' nor as round and fleshy as the Africans'. Why did early humans develop different nose tips in different continents?

MY THEORIES AND INTERPRETATIONS: The development of nose characteristics among different groups of people has a lot to do with the climate in each continent. In Europe, it was very cold, particularly during the time when early humans migrated to Europe, which occurred during the Ice Age. Winters were long with blizzards. Summers were short with cold rain from the Atlantic Ocean. People often caught colds (we all know that we often catch colds in the winter time). When one person had a cold, he or she spreads it to others. It is reasonable to predict that early humans in Europe had colds frequently. When you have a cold, you will have a runny nose. What do you do when your nose is running? You blow it. How do we blow our noses? We either use the fingers of both hands to press the nose from both sides or the thumb and index finger of one hand to squeeze the nose from both sides to make the nasal cavity narrower, and then we give it a good blow. The nose is formed of cartilage and soft tissues. Cartilage is what we call soft bone. It is flexible and may be altered in shape over time if under repeated pressure. Early European people had to press their noses from both sides with pressure frequently while they blew their noses, which made the nose narrower and pushed the nose bridge higher. Year after year, generation after generation, this action caused early humans in Europe to develop high and narrow noses. Eventually, this new nose characteristic became genetic among Europeans. Once it became genetic, all European descendants inherit the trait of high and narrow noses no matter where they are born in the world today.

Luckily for early humans in Europe, their narrow and high noses led to a narrower nasal passage, which helped to slow down the air entering the nostrils, allowing more time for the nose to warm up the cold air before it entered the sensitive lungs. This modification of the nasal passage helped early humans adapt to the cold climate in Europe, resulting in fewer colds among their descendants.

The climate was not the same across the continent of Europe. Some places were colder with worse weather than other places. People who lived in those geographic areas may have had colds more often and blew their noses more frequently. Consequently, they pushed their nose bridges up so high that they arched to form hooked noses. This is why some Europeans have arched or hooked noses. Although hooked noses are a genetic trait that will pass down to descendants, not all children will inherit this gene.

There are some other characteristics of Europeans' noses. Their noses are usually very lean, with little fatty tissue. This resulted from pressing their noses frequently from both sides when blowing their noses, which prevented any accumulation of fatty tissue. Europeans also have pointed nose tips, slightly pointing downward. This was also a result of how they blew their noses. Let's think about what you usually do after you blow your nose. You usually slide your fingers down both sides of the nose to the nose tip to squeeze all the fluid out of the nasal cavity. When you do that all the time, you are pulling the nose tip downward. This was how European people developed pointed nose tips, lean and slightly pointing downward. This type of nose tip is also genetic. Whether it belongs to the same gene as the high and narrow noses or a different gene, it doesn't matter. The fact is that these unique noses and nose tips distinguish Europeans from all other groups of people.

In Africa, the climate was hot because it was situated on both sides of the equator. Early humans seldom caught colds. They didn't have to blow their noses frequently. This is why they didn't develop high and narrow noses like Europeans. However, they had another problem. They sweat a lot because of the hot climate. In the equatorial area of Africa, the daytime temperature likely reached 100° Fahrenheit (38° C) or higher. Under the hot sun, sweat poured down from people's faces. They did not have air-conditioning or fans like we have today. Early humans constantly had to wipe sweat from their faces. They did not have cloths or tissue paper then, so they used their bare hands to wipe the sweat from their foreheads down over their faces. This motion pressed the nose bridge downward unconsciously. When they pressed their nose bridges downward repeatedly, daily, year after year, it changed the cartilage of the nose bridge to become low and wide or flat. After many generations, low and wide noses became genetic among African people. Once it became genetic, their descendants will have low and wide noses, even if they are born in a cold-climate continent.

By wiping sweat downward from the forehead and over the nose, the hand also pushed the fatty tissues in the nose down toward the nose tip. Consequently, African people developed round and fatty nose tips. Why do some African people have flat, slightly upward-facing nose tips? This was probably attributed to how they wiped the sweat dripping down from their nose tips. Quite commonly, we use the backs of our hands or arms to wipe the sweat beneath the nose tip by wiping upward, particularly when both hands are dirty or holding something. This motion pushed the nose tip up, and it also flattened it. This was how the African people developed rounded, flat, front-facing or tilted up, fleshy nose tips. Again, such traits were passed down to their descendants.

However, not all African people have low and wide or flat noses with round nose tips. Africa is a very large continent. In places farther away from the equator or at a higher altitude, the climate was much cooler with occasional snow. People didn't develop low and wide noses because they did not sweat as much due to the cooler climate. Early humans who lived in those areas of Africa developed slightly higher and narrower noses.

In addition, even though nose traits are genetic, their characteristics are changeable due to the soft and flexible nature of nose cartilage. If a climate change continued for a few hundred years, then there would be a noticeable change of nose characteristics. For example: many African people who migrated to Europe and North America a few hundred years ago developed noticeably higher and narrower noses than people in Africa due to having more colds and blowing their noses more frequently in a colder climate. Therefore, there are great variations in nose characteristics among African people.

In Asia, the climate was warm with four seasons of different weather, particularly in northern Asia. People also caught colds in the wintertime and had to blow their noses—but not as often as the Europeans. They also sweat in the summertime and had to wipe the sweat from their faces—but again, not as often as the Africans. Consequently, they developed medium-size noses that are not as high and narrow as the Europeans and not as low and wide as the Africans. Their noses have more fatty tissues than the Europeans but not as much as the Africans. Their nose tips are neither pointing downward nor facing upward. This type of nose and nose tip also became genetic among Asian people.

Southeast Asia is a tropical and equatorial climate—hot and humid. People sweat a lot more. They often pressed their noses downward while wiping sweat from their faces. Consequently, people in Southeast Asia have slightly lower and wider noses with more fatty tissues than people in northern Asia. Some have noses very similar to African people. Note: nose characteristics are mixed among Southeast Asians due to a large population of Chinese descendants whose ancestors migrated to Southeast Asia several hundred years ago.

SUMMARY: Climate has played a major role in the development of different types of noses. The European people's high and narrow noses with lean and pointed nose tips were formed due to living in cold environments, whereas the African people's low and wide noses with rounded and fleshy nose tips were developed in hot climates. Asian people's noses, which were developed in mild and seasonal climates, fit perfectly into the gap between the noses of Europeans and Africans. Together, they form a perfect linear change of nose appearance among these three groups of people. They fully support my theory that nose traits were attributed to the climate in which people lived.

Europe, Asia, and Africa had totally different climates. Consequently, the people of each continent developed different characteristics of noses and nose tips. Nevertheless, they were not an adaptation. They were formed as a result of people's daily habits and behaviors in response to the climate in which they lived. Over time, the new characteristics became genetic among each group of people. This occurred naturally and unconsciously. However, the narrow noses of European people unexpectedly helped them to adapt to a cold climate, which aided their survival in Europe because the narrower nasal passage gave more time to warm up the cold air before it entered the lungs.

2.2

NOSTRILS

FACTS AND QUESTIONS: The nostrils are a part of the nose. However, they have their own characteristics. Early humans developed different types of nostrils in different continents. European people have narrow nostrils, slightly facing downward. Their nostrils are usually not visible at eye level. Why didn't Europeans have large round nostrils? An artist can easily sketch a large round nostril on both sides of a high nose.

African people have large round nostrils, facing front or slightly upward, which are easily visible from eye level. Why do African people have large round nostrils? This feature does not coincide with their low and wide noses. Chapter 2.1—NOSES states that the development of low and wide noses among Africans was due to pressing down the nose bridge while wiping the sweat from their faces. They could easily have pressed their nostrils down at the same time to make them narrow, lying flat along the face. Why didn't they have narrow nostrils lying flat along the face?

Asians have oval nostrils, which are smaller and narrower among northern Asians and gradually become larger and more round among Southeastern Asians. Why do Asian people have oval nostrils? Why did Asians' nostrils change in size and shape from north to south?

MY THEORIES AND INTERPRETATIONS: Human bodies must maintain a constant temperature, which is 98.6° F (37° C). A few degrees too high, you will run a fever. A few degrees below that, you will feel chill or go into hypothermia. On hot, sunny days or when we exercise or do physical work, we dissipate our body heat through perspiration. On normal days, however, we rely on our nostrils to maintain a constant body temperature. The nostrils are the openings connecting the inside of our bodies to the outside. When we inhale, we bring in oxygen through our nostrils into our lungs, and when we exhale, carbon dioxide leaves the body. At the same time, our nostrils also regulate our internal body temperature with the outside air while we breathe. They provide twenty-four-hour ventilation. This is similar to the windows in our homes. Before we had air-conditioning or heating systems, we used windows to adjust the temperature of our houses. We kept windows closed in the wintertime to keep the heat inside and to prevent cold air from entering the house. We opened windows wide in the summertime to let the heat out and allow the cool breeze in to cool down the house. We adjusted the window opening according to the weather condition and the temperature we desired. But how do we close or open our nostrils? Human bodies are amazing. We have developed different types of nostrils of different sizes and shapes to control the ventilation of our bodies, so we could adapt to the climate we lived in.

In Europe, the continent was so cold that early humans covered their entire bodies with thick clothing (likely furs and skins from animals) and fur hats on their heads to stay warm. However, they could not cover their noses because they needed to breathe.

If they had big and round nostrils, then they would lose too much body heat through them, and cold air would rush into their lungs, causing a severe cold or pneumonia. To avoid that, they must have narrow nostrils to allow them to breathe, to keep body heat inside, and to slow down the cold air entering their lungs.

Europeans had naturally developed narrow nostrils, attributed to blowing their noses frequently due to having colds. When they frequently squeezed their noses from both sides with their fingers, the nostrils naturally became narrower. Just having narrow nostrils might not be sufficient to prevent losing body heat if the openings were facing upward because hot air escaped quickly upward. They needed nostril openings facing downward, which again were formed naturally among early humans in Europe because they pulled the nose tip down while squeezing all the fluid out of the nose. When the nostrils were facing downward, hot body air could not escape quickly. There was another benefit of downward-facing nostrils. When people breathe, hot body air exhaled downward to keep their lips warm. This was particularly important to females because they did not have mustaches to keep the area above their lips warm. This is truly a remarkable design of how the human body has developed nostrils to adapt to the cold climate in Europe. In southern Europe by the Mediterranean Sea, people's nostrils are not as narrow as northern Europeans due to the warmer climate.

These kinds of downward-facing narrow nostrils became genetic among early humans in Europe, which has helped their descendants to survive in cold climates. Along with other adaptations, Europeans grew to a population of more than one billion people (almost half of them have migrated to other areas of the world). Today, Europeans have downward-facing, narrow nostrils because of the genes they have inherited.

In Africa, it was hot and humid. People needed to cool down their bodies. If they had narrow and small nostrils, then the hot air inside their bodies would not be able to escape quickly. Their bodies would easily overheat and not function efficiently. This is why Africans do not have narrow nostrils that lie flat along the face, despite their ancestors having constantly pressed the nostrils down while they wiped the sweat from their faces. They needed big and round nostrils to let the hot internal air leave their bodies freely and quickly to help with cooling. If their nostrils were facing downward, then the hot air could not disperse easily because hot air rises instead of going down. This is why early humans in Africa developed big round or oval round nostrils that face front and sometimes slightly upward to help cool their bodies, so they could adapt to the hot climate in which they lived. This was the cooling mechanism of early humans in Africa before the invention of electric fans and air-conditioning. These types of nostrils became genetic among Africans, so their children could cope with the hot weather as well. Today, Africans still have these types of nostrils, even if they were born outside of Africa.

However, in areas away from the equator and at a higher altitude, such as the Ethiopia Highlands, the weather was much cooler. Big round nostrils would not be suitable because people would catch colds and lose too much body heat. Instead, early humans who lived in cooler areas developed oval or narrower nostrils, and so did their descendants. Therefore, there are variations in nostrils among African people. It all depends on where their ancestors lived in Africa.

In Asia, the climate changed from cold in the northern area to very hot in the equatorial area. Early humans in Asia also developed their nostrils differently in different regions to adapt to the climate in which they lived. In northern Asia, people developed oval or pear-shaped nostrils, slightly facing downward, which allowed them to keep their body heat inside during wintertime and to disperse the hot body air in summertime. As the climate became hotter in southern China, people's nostrils also changed to a bigger size. In Southeast Asia, the climate was hotter and more humid. It was necessary for people to disperse the hot air through the nostrils quickly. They developed more rounded, bigger nostrils, slightly facing front, to adapt to the hot and humid climate. In some eastern islands of Indonesia and New Guinea, situated just south of the equator, the natives developed nostrils very similar to African people due to a similar climate to Africa.

Today, there are many travelers and migrants in different regions of Asia. You will see many different sizes and shapes of nostrils among Asians. Oval and pear-shaped nostrils are most common, which are genetic among Asian people. If you observe carefully, then you will notice that round and big nostrils become more common among people in Southeast Asia due to the hotter climate.

SUMMARY: The development of different shapes and sizes of nostrils were early humans' adaptation to the climates in which they lived, so they could survive and live better. The modification of nostrils formed naturally, slowly, and unconsciously. All species in the wild have the capability of changing their bodies to make themselves more fit for a new environment. For example: sea lions were four-legged land mammals millions of years ago. When they moved from the land to the ocean for food, they had to gradually change their bodies to adapt to aquatic life by changing their legs to flippers to help them swim faster. They also increased their body fat to keep them warm and insulated from the cold Arctic water. Human beings are no exception. We are also capable of changing our bodies to adapt to our environments. Since these changes are slow and gradual, we are not aware of them.

After the early Europeans gradually evolved their nostrils to a narrower and smaller size, they may have caught fewer colds and become healthier because the cold air could not rush into their noses quickly, and their nasal cavities and passages had more time to warm up the cold air before it entered the lungs. In Africa, early humans may have also reduced their body heat and sweating because of changing their nostrils to a larger size, more rounded, and slightly facing upward, which made it easier for internal hot air to disperse. In Asia, even though there were no extreme climates like in Europe and Africa, people still had to change their nostrils to different sizes and shapes to adapt to the variable and seasonal climate. Thus, they lived better, and their population multiplied.

Today, when you look at the nostrils of European and African people, they look very different from each other. The fact is that the narrow nostrils of European people were developed to adapt to the cold climate in Europe, whereas the round nostrils of African people was developed to adapt to the hot climate in Africa. The oval nostrils of the Asian people were developed to adapt to the seasonal and mild climate in Asia. If you put the oval nostrils of the Asian people in between the Europeans' narrow nostrils and the Africans' round nostrils, then they form a gradual change of nostrils among these three groups of people. In other words, the same group of early humans developed different nostrils in Europe, Asia, and Africa, attributable to the different climates in these three continents.

2.3

EYE SIZE

FACTS AND QUESTIONS: When we look at the eyes of different groups of people, we have an impression that the eyes of European people are bigger by far than the eyes of African and Asian people. Asians have the smallest eyes among the three. The truth is that human eyes are remarkably similar in size among all groups of people (Wikipedia). The different eye sizes we see are external views of the eyes. The eyeballs are generally about the same size. What makes the eyes small or large is the opening of the eye window and the capability of opening the eyelids. Why do European people have the largest eyes (external view)?

Most interesting of all is the slender eyes of many Asian people, particularly those of Chinese, Korean, Japanese, and Mongolian origin. This is unique to Asian people. If a person has slender eyes, then you almost know for sure that he or she has Asian lineage. Why do Asian people have small and narrow eyes? No one has ever proposed an acceptable theory or a reasonable explanation for this unique trait. Another puzzle is why only northern Asians have slender eyes. When you go to countries in Southeast Asia, most people there do not have slender eyes except for those who are descendants of early Chinese migrants.

MY THEORIES AND INTERPRETATIONS: Let's go back to the time when early humans migrated to Europe, about forty-five thousand years ago during the glacial period. The weather was extremely cold. Most of them lived in caves, most likely limestone caverns, which can be found throughout Europe. Many caverns were very large and spacious. A group of people could live together and have space to store the prey they brought back from hunting. Others lived in log cabins or huts made of tree branches covered with evergreen needles or other natural materials (hereinafter collectively referred to as shelters). They likely stayed inside their shelters most of the time because of the bitter cold outside. You could almost imagine that their shelters were very dark inside. Sunlight couldn't reach the inside of the caverns. The dim light they might have had came from burning wood branches, torches, or oil lamps (in later days). They couldn't open doors (if they stayed in a hut or cabin) to let sunlight in because the cold air would rush into their shelters. When they were inside, they strove for more light to see better. Naturally, they opened their eyes wide to enhance their vision. That's what we usually do in a dark place. Explanation: what we can see is the amount of light that enters into our eyes through the pupil (the dark circular spot in the center of eye). Too bright a light will cause blurred vision, whereas darkness reduces your vision. Our pupil can change its size (controlled by iris) to control the amount of light entering the eyes. When you are in a dark place, you open your eyes wide, so no part of the pupil and iris is covered. As the pupils open fully, you will be able to see better in a dark area. When you go out into the bright sun, your pupils decrease the opening to limit the amount of light entering to reduce the glare. It is reasonable to predict that early Europeans had to keep their eyes wide open while they were inside their dark shelters. Over time, they were able to lift up their eyelids completely and open the eyes wide. Consequently, they developed bigger eyes (external view). The trait of big eyes with fully movable eyelids became genetic among Europeans. All their descendants have inherited this trait, even though they are no longer living in dark shelters.

In Africa, early humans also lived in dark shelters. However, they spent very little time inside their shelters because of the hot climate. They rarely had to keep their eyes wide opened. Consequently, they have not developed big eyes like the European people. It is reasonable to predict that the eyes of African people today may be very similar to the eyes of early humans in Ethiopia 195,000 years ago.

In Asia, people in China, Korea, Japan, and Mongolia have developed slender eyes. This is truly a mystery. Why does this large group of people, almost one fifth of the world's population, have slender eyes that distinguish them from all other groups of people? There are many theories. Some believe that it was the desert environment in China, where dust storms caused people to squint their eyes, resulting in narrow eyes. This theory does not coincide with the geography of China. There are no deserts in the populated areas of China, and neither are there large deserts in Korea and Japan. Dust storms occur a few times a year only in the northern area of China. Others say that their slender eyes resulted from the bitter cold in China that caused people to close their eyes slightly. If that were the cause of slender eyes, then Europeans should have narrower eyes than Chinese because of living in a much colder climate. Let's make the story short: Asians' slender eyes remain a mystery in anthropology.

I have developed a theory that the slender eyes of the northern Asian people were developed as a result of their hairstyles. You may be wondering why how hairstyles have anything to do with eye traits. Here is my interpretation: China has a long history of civilization. The first kingdom dates back to four thousand years ago and might be as early as sixty-five hundred years ago (according to Sarah Pruitt, published on the Internet). As culture and civilization developed, people learned how to dress well and to comb their hair. Traditionally, Chinese men combed their hair back from their faces, pulling the hair tight to make a knob or bun-shaped hairstyle on top of their heads. (You can see this hairstyle among the terracotta warriors buried in the tomb of the First Emperor of China date 210 BC.) Women did the same, but sometimes they had long braids or ponytails. When they tightly pulled the hair on both sides of the head back and up at a 45° angle, they also pulled the skin at the corner of both eyes up 45°. This made their eyes slender as well as restricted the movement of their eyelids. You can do a simple experiment to test this theory: put your hands over both temples and pull the skin tight toward the hairline. You will find that you can't open your eyes wide or move the upper eyelids. Your eyes become slender. The Chinese wore this hairstyle for thousands of years (possibly even long before civilization), which constantly restricted the movement of their eyelids day and night. Over such a long time of restraint, their eyes became narrower and smaller. This is also the cause of their inclined eyes (slanted eyes), with the eye corners slightly tilted upward toward the hairline. The eyelids thus lost their mobility and could not open fully. Over time, slender eyes became genetic among Chinese people.

Why do Korean, Japanese, and Mongolian people have the same eye traits? The story goes back to two thousand years ago. The first emperor of China, who built the Great Wall of China, ended the war among the Warring States and unified China into one large country. He greatly expanded the territory of China, making it the largest country in Central Asia (the name China means "the country in the center"). Although his reign did not last long, China continued to be the superior country in Asia for two thousand years. All the surrounding countries, such as Korea, Japan, and Mongolia, were smaller and less populated. They viewed China as the heavenly kingdom and the Chinese king as being the heavenly king. They came to China to learn culture, literature, architecture, and agriculture, as well as the Chinese hairstyle. Thus, all the people of Korea, Japan, and Mongolia had the same hairstyle as the Chinese people. This hairstyle has continued for two thousand years in Japan as seen among Japanese Samurai warriors and Geisha girls. (See chapter 6 for more on the Chinese migration to Japan.) Even today, the Sumo wrestlers still wear the traditional Chinese hairstyle. Consequently, they all have developed slender eyes, which also became a genetic trait among Japanese, Korean, and Mongolian people.

You may argue that many European girls wear ponytail hairstyles today. Why don't they have slender eyes? We must remember that genetic slender eyes were developed as a result of restrained eye movement over thousands of years, not because of once-in-a-while hairdressing. Besides, it is reasonable to predict that European women did not wear ponytails during the Ice Age because it would have been too cold to wear their hair up. They likely kept their hair down to help keep their necks and shoulders warm. Therefore, their eyes have not been restrained for thousands of years like the Chinese people.

Why did the people in Southeast Asia have larger eyes than northern Asians? Why didn't they have slender eyes? This is because they did not wear the same hairstyle as the Chinese people. They let their hair down instead of pulling it tight and up to make a knob on top of their heads. Their eyelids could open freely and were not restrained in movement. This is why they did not develop slender eyes. Consequently, they have larger eyes than northern Asian people. The reason that Southeast Asians did not wear the traditional Chinese hairstyle is because they have not been influenced by Chinese culture. For centuries, Chinese rulers tried hard to maintain control over central and northern China. They considered southern China as southern barbarian states, and Southeast Asia was far from their reach. It wasn't until five hundred years ago that China (during the Ming Dynasty) expanded its trade in Southeast Asia and Europe. Since then, a large population of southern Chinese people migrated to Southeast Asia. The people you see there who have slender eyes are usually descendants of early Chinese migrants.

SUMMARY: European people's big eyes (external view) were developed by adapting to a dark environment. They had to open their eyes wide and big to enhance their vision in their dark shelters, which caused a genetic change to their eyes over time. The slender eyes of central and northern Asian people were developed because of their traditional hairstyle, which restricted the opening of the eyelids. However, it is believed that the gene of slender eyes is regressing, as Asian people have abandoned the traditional Chinese hairstyle over the last one hundred years. Their eyes have the freedom to grow bigger, and their eyelids are no longer restrained. In the recent century, the eyes of northern and central Asian people have grown considerably bigger, and slender eyes have become less common. Their future generations will have even bigger eyes with more movable eyelids. Slender eyes will only be seen among babies and young children. As they grow older, their eyes will change to a bigger size. African and Southeast Asian people have not changed their eye sizes because there was no change in climate, culture, and lifestyle. In other words, if Europe was not so cold that it caused people to stay inside their dark shelters, and if Asians did not wear their traditional hairstyle for thousands of years, then all people in these three continents would likely have similar-size eyes.

2.4

EYE COLOR

FACTS AND QUESTIONS: Eye color comes from the color of the irises (the colored area surrounding the pupil in the center of eye). The universal eye color is brown, varying from light brown to dark brown. Some European people have unique blue and green eyes that distinguish them from all other groups of people.

The color of the iris is not a single uniform color. Generally, it is a mix of different shades of colors, radiating from the pupil in the center of the eye, and each color can vary from light to dark. There are many different eye colors among Europeans. Generally, you will see more blue and green eyes in northern Europe and more greenish-brown or light-brown eyes in southern Europe. Why does eye color change in different regions of Europe? If you searched the Internet for why Caucasian people have blue and green eyes, you will not find a clear and definite answer. Most people think it is related to their white skin and low pigmentation. It is true that our eye color is made of melanin (a natural pigment in the human body). The questions are why do Europeans have blue and green irises, and why do African and Asian people have dark-brown eyes?

Some scientists have used DNA and genetic mutation to explain this puzzle, which made it more difficult to understand. Others believe that people have different eye color because we came from different ancestral lineages. Most people believe it is genetic, without questioning how the gene developed before it became a genetic trait. No one has ever answered exactly how and why the gene developed at the beginning. The truth is that the color of human eyes remains a mystery.

MY THEORIES AND INTERPRETATIONS: I believe that blue and green eyes were developed among early Europeans to help them see better in their dark shelters. It is best to explain my theory by starting with the purpose of the iris. The pupil provides our sight, so why do we even need the iris? Let me give you an analogy. The pupil is like a window, whereas the iris is like the curtain around the window. What we see outside a house is what we see through the window. The iris can control the opening of the pupil just like we can open and close the curtain to control the size of the window and the amount of light entering the room. We also use different-colored curtains to get the most desirable amount of light we'd like to have. For example: light-colored curtains allow more light into the room, whereas dark-colored curtains block bright light and make the room darker. The color of the iris serves the same purpose. A light-colored iris, such as blue and green, allows more light into your eyes, which helps you see better in a dark environment. A dark-colored iris, such as dark brown, blocks the sunlight, which helps you decrease the glare and reduce blurred vision in a bright light environment.

As described in section 2.3—EYE SIZE, early humans in Europe spent much time inside dark shelters due to the bitter cold outside. While they were inside, they had to open their eyes wide to let more light into the pupil, so they could see better. However, it was still insufficient to increase their vision, particularly when early Europeans still had dark-brown irises that blocked most of the light. (We must remember that early Europeans migrated from Africa. They likely had dark-brown eyes like many other African people.) It was necessary for them to change the irises to a lighter color to allow more light in. It is just like we change a curtain to a lighter color when we want more light in a room. Blue and green irises allow more light into the pupil and help increase vision in a dimly lit place. This was why early humans in Europe gradually changed their irises to a lighter color by replacing the dark-brown irises with blue or green to adapt to the dark environment inside their shelters.

Of course, this adaptation was gradual and took time. Since the color of our irises was made of radiating rays of different colors, it allowed people to get the exact amount of light they needed for their vision by adjusting the proportion of each color. Whether they chose a blue or green hue, it would depend on how dark their shelters were and how long they spent inside every year. If people had to stay in a very dark environment for a long time, then it is likely they would develop blue irises. In a medium-dark environment, they likely developed green irises. In southern Europe, people stayed in their shelters less because of the warmer climate. They did not live in a totally dark environment. Consequently, they adopted greenish-brown or light-brown irises, which were more suitable for their vision needs. These were the reasons that early humans in Europe developed different light-colored irises. Among these colors, there were bluish green, greenish brown, and so on, for different environments. This is truly an amazing design of the human eye. After many generations, blue, green, and light-brown eyes became genetic traits among European people. Mixed marriages among Europeans from different regions gave their descendants many different-colored irises, resulting in a great diversity of eye color among Europeans.

In Africa and Asia, people stayed outdoors most of the time because of the hot climate. The sunlight was bright and intense. They needed dark-colored irises to reduce the amount of sunlight entering their eyes. This is why they developed dark-brown irises. If they adopted blue or green irises, then they would have blurred vision, and their eyes would be damaged by the bright sunlight because light-colored irises allow too much sunlight passing through. It is reasonable to predict that a dark-brown iris was also the eye color of early humans 195,000 years ago before they left their originated ground in Ethiopia, because Ethiopia was located in the equatorial area with a high intensity of sunlight. When early humans migrated to Asia and other places in Africa, they kept their dark-brown irises, which worked well in the new settlement area. There was no need to adopt another eye color other than to increase or decrease the shade of brown.

Today, it is common for European people to wear sunglasses because the sunlight is too bright for their blue and green eyes. You will also notice that most sunglasses are dark brown, as this color can block most of the sunlight and still provide good vision. You seldom see any local people in Southeast Asia, Africa, or the Caribbean Islands wearing sunglasses, even on a bright sunny day. The fact is that they don't need to—they already have a pair of sunglasses inside their eyes. The dark-brown irises of Asian and African people were a gift from their ancestors. They all got a pair of built-in sunglasses with a lifetime warranty.

SUMMARY: Most of the world's population has dark-brown eyes. The blue and green eyes of European people were obviously different from all other groups of people. No wonder some people thought they had come from different ancestors. The truth is that this unique trait was simply developed to adapt to the dark environment inside their shelters. Their prolonged living in dark shelters was enforced by the cold climate in Europe.

Similar adaptation also occurred in many species in the wild kingdom. Most daytime feeding and grazing animals, such as deer and horses, have dark-brown or black eyes. Just like humans, they also need dark-colored irises to reduce the bright sunlight and to protect their eyes. In contrast, nighttime hunters, such as owls, cats, and tigers, have adopted light-colored irises to increase their vision, so they can hunt in the dark of night. They cannot have dark-brown irises, which will make them as blind as their prey. Owls have developed big round eyes with large pupils in the center because large pupils allow more light to enter their eyes. Owls also chose light-colored irises (usually yellow) to let in dim light to help increase their vision in the dark. Their irises are so big that they cover the entire eye. Without making these changes, owls would not be able to see or hunt at night.

As you can see, the reasons that early humans in Europe developed bigger eyes and blue or green irises coincide with each other. Both helped them to adapt to a dark environment. If Europe had not been frigidly cold for most of the year and forced early humans to stay inside their dark shelters, then they would not have developed bigger eyes or blue or green irises. They would have dark-brown eyes like all other groups of people.

A distribution map of light-colored eyes in and near Europe ("Why do Europeans have so many hair and eye colors?" Peter Frost, http://cogweb.ucla.edu/ep/Frost) shows the highest concentration in the Baltic Sea region (Norway, Sweden, and Finland). More than 80 percent of people in that region have light-colored eyes. The percentage frequency decreases southward toward the Mediterranean Sea. Although this is a modern-day distribution map, it likely represents the same distribution of light eyes of early humans in Europe, since eye colors are genetic. Assuming that Frost's data are correct, his map strongly supports my theory that blue and green irises were developed to adapt to a dark environment. Explanation: the Baltic Sea was the coldest region in Europe during the Ice Age. In other words, most inhabitants likely had to stay inside their dark caverns to avoid the cold outside. Due to continuous living inside dark shelters, early humans had to develop light-colored irises to increase their vision inside their dark caverns. As a result, most of the population of early humans in the Baltic Sea region developed blue or green eyes. Moving southward toward the Mediterranean Sea where the weather was warmer, the light-eyed population decreased and was gradually replaced by light-brown and brown eyes. Because people in warmer regions did not have to live inside dark shelters all the time, they had less need for light-colored irises. (Note: Peter Frost has a different hypothesis of the development light-colored eyes among Europeans, which is described and discussed in section 2.15—HAIR COLOR.)

2.5

EYELIDS

FACTS AND QUESTIONS: Eyelids protect our eyes from injury by foreign objects, such as dirt, dust, and debris. When they close and open, they spread tears over the eyeball, helping our eyes stay moist and comfortable. There are many different types of eyelids among different groups of people, even though they all serve the same purposes. European people have the largest and fully movable upper eyelid, whereas Asian people have the smallest eyelid with little mobility. African people have medium-size eyelids, which are in between the Europeans and Asians. Why did people of different continents develop different eyelids? Why did northern Asian people develop small and immovable eyelids?

Asian and African people's eyes are situated outward, slightly outside the eye socket. The eyes of European people are situated inside the eye socket, which makes the eyebrow bone more pronounced and causes it to hang over the eyes. This appearance causes some Europeans to have slightly sunken eyes. Why do the eyeballs sit differently among different groups of people?

MY THEORIES AND INTERPRETATIONS: Early humans in Europe developed big eyes with blue and green irises to adapt to the dark environment of their shelters. (Details are provided in the previous two sections.) However, this adaptation created a problem. When they went outside on sunny days, the bright sunlight was too strong and intense for their blue and green eyes, which let too much light pass through the irises. The strong sunlight caused damage to their eyes and blurred their vision. It was worse during wintertime. When the ground was covered with snow, the reflection increased the glare, causing snow blindness. What could they do about this problem? Of course, they didn't have sunglasses to reduce the sunlight like we have today. However, the human body tended to recognize things that might be harmful to it. It would make changes to adapt to the new environment. It started to move the eyeballs gradually inward into the eye socket, which gave the eyes some shade from the eyebrow bone (the bone that protrudes above the eye socket). This is similar to when we are standing outside on a hot and sunny day, we move closer to the building to get some shade from the overhanging roof. This is why European people have slightly sunken eyes. Even thought it was just a slight inward move of the eyeball's position, it gave some relief to their eyes from the bright sunlight. At the same time, their eyes also got some shade from their high nose bridges when the sunlight came from the side.

Another change was the development of big upper eyelids. Early humans in Europe gradually developed big moveable eyelids to protect their big eyes, which otherwise would be totally exposed. The big eyelids helped them to block the intense sunlight. They were fully moveable and could open completely when they needed more light to enhance their vision in their dark shelters. When they were outside, they could close them or partially open them, depending on the intensity of sunlight. Some people also developed secondary small eyelids at the bottom of the big upper eyelid to allow for adjustment of brightness as needed. It is not unusual to have double upper eyelids. In the animal kingdom, owls have three sets of eyelids. Each has a different purpose and function.

But big upper eyelids created a small problem. The eyelid is a thin layer of skin. When you lifted up the eyelid to fully open your eyes, it formed wrinkles above the eye. This was not pretty. The human body seems to be able to recognize every little detail and thus made adjustments accordingly during the eyelid's adaptation. Instead of leaving wrinkled skin outside, the body retracted the skin inward to hide it underneath the roof of the eye socket. It hid the eyelid skin and protected the eyeball from rubbing against the roof of the eye socket. This is why there is a distinct crease at the top of the upper eyelid below the eyebrow. Women usually wear darker eye makeup to emphasize this crease, making their eyelids more distinct and bigger. Big upper eyelids seemed to be more common among European women than men because they had bigger eyes due to spending more time inside dark shelters.

In southern Europe, early humans spent less time in their dark shelters because of the warmer climate. They had adopted brown eyes, which might contain some shades of blue and green. They did not develop big upper eyelids like the northern Europeans because their brown eyes are less susceptible to bright sunlight.

In Asia, people of Chinese, Korean, Japanese, and Mongolian origin have small eyelids. Their eyelids have very little mobility. It means that they cannot lift up the upper eyelids to fully open their eyes. This is another human mystery. However, if you know what caused slender eyes among Asian people (see section 2.3—EYE SIZE for details), then this mystery can be answered easily. Asian people's small eyelids with little mobility were attributable to the traditional Chinese hairstyle. When they combed their hair back and pulled it tight and up at a 45° angle to make a knob or bun-shaped hairstyle on top of their heads, they also pulled the skin at both sides of the eye corners tight toward the hairline. It restricted the movement of the upper eyelids, leaving a narrow opening for the eyes to see. Over time, the mobility of the upper eyelids decreased and became immovable. The only movable portion was a small lid at the bottom of the upper eyelid, which allowed the eyes to adjust the amount of light entering and to spread tears to moisten the eyes. Some people didn't even have this movable small lid, probably due to stronger restraint and a longer time of restriction. This trait of small eyelids became genetic among central and northern Asian people.

Some people may think that slender eyes with little eyelid mobility reduced Asian people's eyesight somewhat. The truth is that there are more advantages than disadvantages. Their view is the same as any wide-open big eyes. Our sight is what we see through the pupil (the tiny dark spot in the center of the eye). As long as the pupil is not covered, the angle of the view is same. Just imagine you are looking behind a wooden door through a small keyhole. You can see everything behind the door as if the door were not there. Among the advantages, their immovable eyelids protected the eyes from damage by sunlight as well as from dust and debris. Their dark-brown irises helped them reduce the bright sunlight like a pair sunglasses. The only disadvantage was lower vision in dark environments because eyelids covered a part of their irises. However, this did not create a big problem because Asian people lived in dark environments only for a short time because of the warm climate. This is why Asian people, about one fifth of the world's population, have maintained these eye and eyelid traits. Otherwise, slender eyes would have been replaced long ago by a new adaptation. Many people do not know that, historically, slender eyes were considered beautiful in China. Different cultures have different perceptions of beauty. Slender eyes made women more feminine. It also represented the look of the upper class in China as commonly seen in drawings of scholars and government officials.

People in Southeast Asia did not have the same eyelids and slender eyes like central and northern Asians because their ancestors were not influenced by Chinese culture, and they did not wear Chinese traditional hairstyle. As a result, their eyes were larger, and their eyelids were more movable. However, there are variations of eyelids among Southeast Asians because many of them were descendants of Chinese people who had migrated to Southeast Asia hundreds years ago. Some of them were children of mixed marriages between natives and Chinese.

People in Africa have distinct movable eyelids, which are larger than the Asians but smaller than the Europeans. Since they had dark-brown eyes, they didn't need big eyelids to protect their eyes from bright sunlight or to reduce the brightness. Their eyelids likely remained the same since their ancestors settled in Africa.

SUMMARY: Since early Europeans developed bigger eyes and adopted lighter-colored irises to enhance their vision inside their dark shelters, their eyes couldn't tolerate the bright sunlight when they went outside. Large movable eyelids were developed to help early European people adapt to the bright sunlight. They helped them to reduce brightness and blurred vision, and they protected the eyes from damage by sunlight. Otherwise, Europeans might have faced blindness.

Chinese, Korean, Japanese, and Mongolian people have small eyelids with little mobility. They were developed as a result of the traditional Chinese hairstyle. African people's eyelids probably have not changed in size and mobility because there were no extreme changes in climate, environment, or culture since their settlement in Africa. It is reasonable to predict that modern African people's eyelids represent the same trait of early humans in Ethiopia 195,000 years ago.

2.6

EYEBROWS

FACTS AND QUESTIONS: Different groups of people have developed different eyebrows. The most obvious are the blond and light-colored eyebrows of European people, which distinguish them from all other groups of people. Both Asian and African people have black eyebrows. Why did European people have blond or light-colored eyebrows?

Generally, European people have thicker, denser, and longer eyebrows, whereas Asian people have thinner, less dense, and shorter eyebrows. African people's eyebrows are in between the Europeans and Asians. There is a great variation of eyebrows within each group of people. Many females pluck their eyebrows to make them thinner or to change their shape. Thus, it is hard to know the original form of their eyebrows. Why did people of different continents develop different eyebrows?

The purposes and functions of the eyes, noses, ears, and mouth are clear. However, the purposes of eyebrows are obscured. Why do we need eyebrows? The main purpose of eyebrows is to prevent salty sweat from the forehead from running down into the eyes as well as to stop rainwater and dust falling down from above. This is why our eyebrows are an arched shape or inclined to the side; they are designed to direct sweat and water away from the face. Another function of eyebrows is to express our emotion. When we are angry or surprised, our eyebrows lift up. When we are worried or depressed, our eyebrows draw closer to each other, drop, or incline. You can find these interpretations on the Internet. However, you will not find answers to why early humans in Europe developed thicker and longer eyebrows or why northern and central Asians have shorter and looser eyebrows.

MY THEORIES AND INTERPRETATIONS: Why did early humans in Europe develop thick, dense, and longer eyebrows? Early humans in Europe had adopted blue and green irises and developed bigger eyes to enhance their vision in their dark shelters, which became a disadvantage when they went outside in the sun. The bright sunlight was too intense for their light-colored eyes and caused blurred vision. They had to squint all the time. Their bodies developed big movable eyelids (see section 2.5—EYELIDS for details) to block the sunlight and control the amount of light entering the eyes. Big eyelids helped them reduce the brightness of the sunlight to a certain degree, but it was not enough. What else could be done? Their bodies grew thicker, denser, and longer eyebrows to reduce the glare of sunlight and provide some shade for their eyes. Explanation: Most Europeans have white-skinned faces, which reflect sunlight and cause more glare to the eyes. Glare makes it difficult for the eyes to see clearly. Longer eyebrows with dense hair can absorb sunlight and reduce glare. Think about American football players, particularly white players, who often paint a black strip underneath their eyes. They do this for the same reason—to reduce the glare from the sun, since they are not allowed to wear sunglasses during the game. Therefore, the development of thicker, denser, and longer eyebrows among early Europeans was an adaptation to bright sunlight.

However, the development of thin, less dense, and short eyebrows of northern and central Asian people (Chinese, Korean, Japanese, and Mongolian) is another story. Their brows developed as a result of their slender eyes. Their dark-brown irises and slender eyes (with eyelids covering most of the eyes) protect their eyes from bright sunlight. There was no need to reduce the glare caused by the sun. Therefore, they did not grow thicker and longer eyebrows. Contrarily, their slender eyes needed more light to help increase their vision. This is why their eyebrows became less dense and shorter—to help increase the brightness. The eyebrows of Southeast Asian people remained the same as their early ancestors, since they did not have slender eyes like the northern Asian people.

Why did European people have light-colored eyebrows, which distinguish them from other groups of people? The scientific literature states that light hair is related to light skin. Light skin is an adaptation to lower levels of sunlight (Wikipedia). In other words, living in a low-sunlight environment caused the development of blond hair. This supports my theory that early humans in Europe lived in their dark shelters for most of the year. They had little exposure to sunlight, because they couldn't stay outside for long, due to the bitterly cold weather. Consequently, they developed light skin, which led to light-colored hair. (See section 2.15—HAIR COLOR for more details.) This is why European people often have blond or light-colored eyebrows. You will find more blond eyebrows among northern Europe people than among southern Europe people—because northern Europeans had to stay in their shelters for a longer time due to the colder climate, leading to lighter skin and lighter hair color.

In Asia and Africa, people lived outdoors most of the time because of the hot climate. They had plenty of sunlight daily. Dark skin was developed to protect them from the intensive sun and ultraviolet (UV) radiation. Dark skin was attributed to abundant eumelanin (a natural pigment in our bodies) in the epidermis, which also causes black hair and eyebrows. Consequently, black hair and black eyebrows became genetic among African and Asian people. (See section 2.12—SKIN COLOR and section 2.15—HAIR COLOR for more details.)

SUMMARY: Most people don't know the purpose and significance of eyebrows. Every little difference in and change to our facial traits has meaning and a story behind it. The development of thicker and longer eyebrows among Europeans was to help them reduce the sun glare, allowing them to adapt to bright sunlight. The short and loose eyebrows of northern and central Asian people were developed to help their slender eyes receive more light so that they had better vision. African people's eyebrows likely remained unchanged, since there was no extreme change of environment or climate in Africa. Therefore, the eyebrows of modern African people may represent the eyebrows of early humans in Ethiopia before they left their originated ground.

2.7

EYELASHES

FACTS AND QUESTIONS: Many modern women use mascara and false eyelashes, which make it difficult to know what their real eyelashes look like. Nevertheless, European people have the longest and thickest eyelashes. Asian people (Chinese, Korean, Japanese, and Mongolian) have thin and short eyelashes. African people have eyelashes in between the Europeans and Asians. Why did people develop different types of eyelashes in different continents? Why do Asian people have the shortest and thinnest eyelashes among these three groups of people?

European people also have unique light-colored eyelashes that distinguish them from Asian and African people. Why do they have light-colored eyelashes, whereas all other groups of people have black eyelashes? Most interesting of all, women of each group of people have longer eyelashes than men. You would think their eyelashes would be the same length, since both men and women lived in the same environment. What causes women to have longer eyelashes than men?

MY THEORIES AND INTERPRETATIONS: We all know that eyelashes protect the eyes from dust and debris. However, most of us do not know that eyelashes also serve to block sun-light and help reduce sun glare. Thick eyelashes shade the irises, thus protecting the eyes from sun damage. This is particularly important to European people who have light-colored eyes. Since early Europeans have developed big eyes and adopted blue and green irises, they have made several changes to help reduce bright sunlight and glare. They have developed big movable eye-lids and grew thick and long eyebrows, which helped to reduce the bright sunlight, but it was still not enough. Thus, they grew thicker and longer eyelashes to reduce more sunlight. These were the combined efforts of early Europeans, who adapted to the bright sunlight outside their shelters. The development of these three traits was slow, gradual, and simultaneous, not one after another. Over time, the new traits became genetic among European people. There are variations of eyelashes among Europeans because of climate differences. Southern Europeans, who lived in a warmer climate and spent less time indoors, developed brown eyes. They had fewer problems with bright sunlight. Consequently, they had shorter eyelashes than those people with blue and green eyes.

Northern and central Asian people had short and thin eye-lashes attributable to their slender eyes with small openings. Unlike Europeans, they did not need long and dense eyelashes to reduce sunlight because they had dark-brown irises that helped reduce sunlight and glare. Since their eyelids covered most part of their eyes, they had less need for long eyelashes to protect the eye from dust and debris. If they grew thick and long eyelashes, then they would not be able to see through their narrow eye openings. Therefore, their eyelashes became short and loose, so they would not block their vision. Southeastern Asians had longer eyelashes because they did not have the slender eyes of northern Asians.

African people likely have kept the same eyelashes as their ancestors in Ethiopia because they have not faced any extreme climate changes like the Europeans or any cultural changes like the Asians.

Why do women have longer eyelashes than men? There is a logical explanation to this phenomenon. Historically, women in all groups of people have a traditional custom of plucking their eyebrows to make them thinner, which makes them more feminine and beautiful. As a result, their eyebrows lost their purposes of reducing sun glare and preventing dust or salty sweat from falling into their eyes. To compensate for this, they grew longer and denser eyelashes. This gene likely developed after the end of the last glacial period. Before then, early humans still lived a hunting and gathering lifestyle. Women probably did not pluck their eyebrows. After the Ice Age (about ten thousand years ago), people started to practice agriculture. As civilization began to develop, their lifestyle improved. Women became more aware of their beauty in all cultures. They started to pluck their eyebrows, which led to the development of longer eyelashes among women.

The development of blond or light eyelashes among European people is similar to the development of light hair, eyebrows, and beards (see section 2.15—HAIR COLOR for more details).

SUMMARY: Sometimes two extremely different environments occur in the same habitat. Many species in the wild must make double adaptations to survive. For example: mountain sheep, bison, and fox grew longer and thicker wool or fur to adapt to the cold weather in the wintertime, and they shed them to adapt to the hot weather in the summertime. A similar situation occurred with early humans in Europe. They developed bigger eyes and changed their irises to blue and green to adapt to the dark environment inside their shelters, and they developed big movable eyelids, grew thicker and longer eyebrows, and longer and denser eyelashes to adapt to the bright sunlight outside. They had to make these changes to allow them to see in both environments; otherwise, they might become blind.

By now, you can see why people of Europe, Asia, and Africa have developed different characteristics of noses, nostrils, eye sizes, eye colors, eyebrows, and eyelashes in each continent. It was because of different climates, shelters, daily habits, cultures, and so on, not because of different ancestral stocks. Their bodies made these changes so that they were more fit for the environments in their new settlement areas, which led to the development of new facial traits and genes. Through heredity, their nose and eye characteristics have been passed down for thousands of years on each continent. Today, their descendants bear the same traits as their ancestors no matter where they were born or live. Consequently, the people of these three continents (Europe, Asia, and Africa) look different from one another, leading to the development of different groups of people or races (as mistaken by early anthropologists).

2.8

LIPS

FACTS AND QUESTIONS: When we talk about facial characteristics, European people are not only known for having blue and green eyes and high and narrow noses but also for having thin lips. Why do European people have thin lips? Another interesting fact is that European men seem to have thinner lips than women. Why?

In Africa, most people have big and full lips. What are the reasons that caused Africans to develop big and full lips? Asian people have lips in between the Europeans and Africans. Each group of people bears a distinct characteristic of lips that distinguishes them from people of another continent. Why did people of different continents develop different types of lips?

The philtrum, the narrow groove extending from the nose to the upper lip, also developed differently among different groups of people. European people seem to have the longest philtrum. As a result, the area between the nose and upper lip is also larger than other groups of people. Why did early humans in Europe develop a long philtrum? Why did African and Asian people have relatively short philtra and narrower spaces between their noses and upper lips?

MY THEORIES AND INTERPRETATIONS: In Europe, the climate was cold and freezing. Before people left their shelters, they bundled up in thick clothes and wore hats to keep warm. They couldn't cover their faces because they needed their eyes to see and their noses to breathe. When they were outside, they immediately closed their mouths tight (a natural response to cold weather) to avoid sucking in cold air and prevent loss of body heat through the mouth. It helped them stay warm and conserve body energy, so they could stay outside longer. Otherwise, they could catch colds and freeze their front teeth. (If the front teeth are exposed to freezing wind for long, then they can become very painful and freeze up.) When people clenched their mouths tight, it was natural that they pulled both lips inward into the mouth. This prevented any cold air from rushing into the mouth and kept their lips warm. If you have experienced a blizzard, then you know that you close your mouth so tight that both lips are totally pulled inside the mouth. The colder it gets, the tighter you clench your lips. This is normal behavior in cold climate. Early humans in Europe had to do that all the time because of the constantly cold weather for most of the year. This habit restrained lip development and prevented any fat accumulation in the lips. Consequently, their lips became thin with little fatty tissue. Thin lips did not make them more fit for cold weather. It was developed unconsciously from their daily habits and behaviors in a cold climate. Over time, Europeans developed thin lips, which eventually became genetic among them. This is why most Europeans have thin lips, particularly those people who lived in colder regions of Europe. However, in southern Europe near the Mediterranean Sea, the climate was warmer. Winter was shorter and not as cold. Early Europeans who lived in those areas did not have to close their mouths tight all the time. Their lips had a chance to be free. Thus, they had medium-size, slightly fuller lips.

If you observe carefully, then you'll notice that European men have thinner lips than women. You would think that they should have the same type of lips, since they both lived in the same climate. Not exactly. Men spent more time outside in the cold than women because of their livelihoods. Men had to close their mouths tight constantly while they were out hunting or gathering, which led to very thin lips. Because women stayed inside their shelters in a slightly warmer environment, they didn't have to hold their lips inside their mouths all the time, resulting in slightly thicker lips. This is why European women have slightly fuller lips than men.

When people closed the mouth tight and pulled the upper lip totally into the mouth, naturally, they also pulled the philtrum longer and enlarged the area between the nose and upper lip. This is why early humans in Europe developed a longer philtrum and a larger area above the upper lip. This feature also became genetic among European people.

In Africa, the climate was very hot. Body temperatures rose quickly. Even though African people had large round nostrils to ventilate the internal hot air, they still need more cooling. It was natural that people had their mouths slightly open to allow more hot body air to exhale quickly and easily. When they let their mouths open, they also let their lips hang loose. This allowed fatty tissues to accumulate in their lips. Consequently, their lips grew bigger and fuller. This development occurred naturally and slowly over time. This trait of full lips became genetic among African people, which is a distinct characteristic of African people, next to their dark skin. However, there are variations of lips among Africans. Those who lived farther away from the equator and in a cooler region have smaller, less full lips. The development of bigger and fuller lips does not make African people more suitable to hot climates. It was developed because of their daily habit and way of life in a hot climate.

African people have a shorter philtrum as a result of this daily habit, since their lips were let loose and free to grow. Their upper lips grew fuller upward, making the philtrum shorter. This is why African people have a narrower area between their noses and upper lips.

In Asia, the climate affected the development of Asians' lips as well. Since the climate in Asia was not as cold as in Europe and not as hot as in Africa, their lips were not as thin as the Europeans and not as big and full as the Africans; the same with their philtra. There are also variations in lips among Asian people in different regions. The climate in the northern area had four seasons of equal length, whereas the southern area had shorter winters and longer summers. As a result, people in northern Asia have thinner lips, whereas southern Asian people have medium-size lips. When you go to Southeast Asia, you will see more people with fuller lips due to living in a tropical climate.

SUMMARY: To develop bigger and fuller lips, your lips must spend considerable time free and loose. The reason early humans in Europe could not develop full lips was because they had to close their mouths tight most of the time due to the freezing cold weather. When the lips were pulled inside the mouth and tightly squeezed, how could they grow big and full? Many European women today like to have fuller lips. Here is an interesting thought. If you allow your lips to be free and loose and leave your mouth slightly open more frequently, then fatty tissue will have a chance to accumulate in the lips. Your lips may grow fuller in time.

Europe, Asia, and Africa represent three extremely different climates of cold, warm, and hot temperatures. Consequently, early humans developed thin lips in Europe because of the cold climate, medium lips in Asia because of the warm climate, and full lips in Africa because of the hot climate. This linear change of lips strongly supports my theory that the development of lips was attributed to the climate in each area. It was developed as a result of people's daily habits and behaviors in response to the climate in which they lived. The development was slow and unconscious. Over time, the lip and philtrum traits became genetic among each group of people. Today, their descendants bear the same traits, even though they were born in a different climate and on a different continent.

2.9

TEETH

FACTS AND QUESTIONS: Whether teeth are a facial trait or not, you can't help but notice people's teeth when they talk or smile. Whether you have good teeth depends on two components. One is your daily habits, and the other is your heredity. Habits, such as eating too much candy or sweets and drinking soda, can cause tooth decay; grabbing a tobacco pipe with your teeth can cause gaps in the teeth; thumb sucking can cause the upper front teeth to protrude. However, crooked and misaligned teeth, weakness of enamel, and resistance to decay are usually genetic.

From general observation, European people seem to have better teeth that are more aligned and show less decay. This may be in part due to the advanced dentistry and dental technology in Europe, and people tend to have more knowledge of how to take care of their teeth. The other part is their genetic factor. Why do Europeans have genetically good teeth? In Asia, poor teeth alignment, tooth decay, and tooth spacing are common problems among Asian people. This was partly due to backward dentistry practices. The other main factor is heredity. Why do Asian people have genetically bad teeth? Asian people also seem to have shorter teeth than European people (based on visual observation). Why do they have shorter teeth?

Buck teeth (protruding upper front teeth) are also common in Asian people, whereas they are rare among European people. What causes buck teeth among Asian people? Why do European people rarely have protruding front teeth?

If you observe carefully, then you will notice that many Japanese people have two relatively large, slightly protruded upper front teeth. This appearance is more noticeable among Japanese women than men. How did Japanese people develop this trait, which is uncommon among other Asians? Note: Japanese protruding teeth are not the same as the buck teeth of other Asian people. Japanese protruding teeth involve only two upper front teeth, whereas the buck teeth of other Asians include several upper front teeth.

MY THEORIES AND INTERPRETATIONS: Asia is the most favorable continent for fruit trees in the world because of its fertile soil and hot climate. It has the largest production of fruits and a great variety. Early humans in Asia had the privilege of eating sweet fruits year-round. Unfortunately, these fruits caused their teeth to decay. Most damaging were the citrus fruits due to their acidic juices, which caused corrosion and wore down the enamel, resulting in smaller and shorter teeth among Asians. In addition, Asians' daily meals consisted of rice, which produced sugar while chewing. Together, their teeth became less resistant to decay. Since Asia is an agricultural continent, farming was Asian people's livelihood. They did not raise cattle for meat or milk, and most people were not able to drink milk daily, leading to weak teeth due to lack of calcium. In the past, humans did not have toothbrushes or the knowledge of brushing teeth. Consequently, they had rotten teeth early in life. Human teeth cannot regenerate or repair themselves. Once they are gone, they are gone forever. A missing tooth leads to spacing. In the olden days, there was no dentistry to repair a missing tooth, which caused other teeth to become crooked. Crooked and misaligned teeth were common among early humans in Asia. This phenomenon occurred in every generation, which eventually became genetic. Therefore, Asian people's bad and shorter teeth were in part hereditary. However, northern Asian people have slightly better teeth than southern Asian people because of fewer varieties and less production of sweet fruits due to a colder northern climate. Their daily meals were mostly wheat products instead of rice, which contained less sugary starch to cause tooth decay.

In Europe, early humans had better teeth because they didn't have the luxury of eating sweet fruits year-round due to the cold climate, which was unfavorable for growing fruit trees. Their daily meals were mostly meat gathered from hunting or fishing. They didn't have any food to cause rapid tooth decay. After the last glacial period in Europe, people started raising sheep or cattle for meat and milk. Their children had more opportunity to drink milk, which led to better teeth due to a sufficient supply of calcium. These are the genetic factors that allowed European people to have better teeth, which became a hereditary trait among them.

Africa is a hot continent but does not produce abundant fruits like Asia, particularly sweet fruits. Therefore, African people had better teeth than Asians. Raising cattle for meat and milk was not a part of their livelihoods. People did not have the chance to drink milk daily, meaning their teeth were likely not as strong as the Europeans due to a lack of calcium.

The buck teeth of Asian people resulted from their eating habits and diet. In Asia, there are plenty of fruits, such as apples, pears, peaches, melons, pineapple, sugarcane, and so on. To eat these fruits, you must bite down with your front teeth, cut, and then tear off a piece. (This is a quick and easy way of eating these fruits without a knife.) This biting habit pulls the front teeth outward. Asian people ate fruits frequently. It caused the protrusion of both the upper and the lower front teeth, but it was more noticeable in the upper front teeth. This became a hereditary trait among some southern Asian people. Although this trait was developed largely due to biting into fruits with their front teeth, you may also consider it an adaptation to eating fruits. Buck teeth help to bite into and cut fruits easier and faster, just like rabbits and squirrels developed bigger and stronger front teeth for fast cutting and biting. Fruits were less available to northern Asian people. As a result, buck teeth were less common among them.

European people had less protruding upper front teeth, which is attributed to the cold weather in Europe. First, early humans in Europe did not have the opportunity to eat fruits daily due to fewer fruit trees in a cold climate. So what caused the Asian people to have buck teeth does not apply to Europeans. Second, Europeans always closed their mouths tight and pulled both lips into the mouth because of the cold weather in Europe (see section 2.8—LIPS for details), thus holding the upper front teeth inward and aligning with the lower front teeth. It is like wearing braces but without braces. This daily habit helped European people to have straight and aligned front teeth.

Many Japanese people have two large, slightly protruding upper front teeth. This appearance is fairly common among Japanese but rarely seen among other Asians. Their protruded upper front teeth are not the same as the buck teeth of other Asian people because Japanese people did not eat fruit daily like the southern Asian people. Japan is located in a colder area of Asia. Fruit production is limited and rare. Therefore, their protruding front teeth are not attributed to eating fruits. What was the cause of their two large protruded upper front teeth?

I believe this trait was a result of Japanese language and its pronunciation. There are many pronunciations in Japanese language that require using the tongue to touch the back of the upper front teeth and to slightly push them outward. For example: "Sa-yo-na-ra" is the Japanese word for good-bye. To pronounce "na-ra," you need to lift the tongue up and to touch the back of the front teeth twice. Each time, you also slightly push the front teeth outward. Another example is the word "arigatou," the Japanese word for thank you. To pronounce "ari" and "tou," your tongue must to touch the back of the front teeth. If their daily conversations required their tongues to touch the back of their upper front teeth and to push them outward frequently, then it likely caused protruded upper front teeth. As teeth are moved slightly outward, it creates space for growing bigger front teeth. This is why Japanese people have two relatively large, slightly protruded upper front teeth.

Historically, Japanese men spoke short sentences with few words, as their traditional culture to show their dignity and high authority, whereas Japanese women might have more conversation at home. Consequently, two large upper front teeth are more common to Japanese women than men due to touching the front teeth more frequently.

SUMMARY: Generally, we believe that climate and environment play an important role in the changing and development of facial and bodily characteristics. We rarely think that a region's diet and eating habits could also play a part in the genetic history of early humans. It is more amazing to know that language could also change the appearance of teeth among a group of people.

The irony is that having so many sweet fruits to eat seemed like a good life for early humans in Asia, but it resulted in a bad hereditary package. Many Asians inherited weak and misaligned teeth from their ancestors; whereas the harsh climate in Europe has actually helped European people to have stronger teeth with aligned front teeth.

2.10

CHEEKS AND CHEEKBONES

FACTS AND QUESTIONS: The cheeks are the fleshy areas on both sides of the face below the eyes. Its upper part has a cheekbone, which lies beneath the eye socket. Although there is not much difference in the cheekbone (the bone itself) between men and women, or among different groups of people, there are distinct differences in the amount of flesh and fatty tissues on the cheekbone, thus forming different traits among cheekbones. If you look carefully, European women have high and prominent cheekbones, which are fleshy, soft, and full. They are usually accompanied by slightly concave cheeks (hollow cheeks), which make the cheekbones more pronounced. European men usually have low and flat cheekbones. Why do European women have higher and fuller cheekbones than men? This difference in cheekbones between men and women is noticeable in all groups of people, not just Europeans. You would think men and women would have the same kind of cheekbone structure, since they both live in the same climate and environment. You may interpret the trait as a characteristic of masculinity or femininity. Whatever it may be, how did the gene develop at the beginning?

African women also have high and prominent full cheeks, but they are not as pronounced as in European women. Why are their cheekbones less prominent than European women? Asian women have even less pronounced cheekbones. Why?

If you search the Internet for answers to why women have developed fleshier and higher cheekbones than men, or why European women have higher and more pronounced cheekbones than African and Asian women, then you will not get a direct answer other than it is a genetic trait. No one could answer exactly how it was developed before it became genetic.

MY THEORIES AND INTERPRETATIONS: I believe that the development of high, fleshy, round, and soft cheekbones among women is related to motherhood. All mothers love their babies. They couldn't stop looking at them, loving them, hugging them, and cuddling them. When you hug a baby, you hold the baby close to your chest and put your cheek close to the baby's head. A baby's head is small, so it fits right to your cheek. As a result, mothers developed slightly concave cheeks to allow more space for their babies' heads. However, if the mother's cheekbone is bony, then it could get painful when rubbing the baby's head. As a result, women started to accumulate more flesh and fatty tissues on the cheekbone to make them round and soft. Together with the hollow cheek, it formed a perfect soft socket for the baby's head, making it more comfortable for both mother and baby. Now, mothers could cuddle their babies longer, and babies fell asleep in their mothers' arms. This explains why women have developed high, round, soft, and fleshy cheekbones with hollow cheeks. It was to make their cheeks a better fit for the baby's head. It became a genetic trait among women of all groups of people.

The reason that men did not have soft and fleshy cheekbones like women was simply that men did not have the time to cuddle the baby like the mothers did. In early days, survival depended on men. Men had to go out gathering, hunting, farming, and so on. They spent most of their time outside their shelters searching for food for the family. They had less time to cuddle babies. Consequently, men's cheekbones remained bony, low, and flat. It also explains why men's cheeks were not as concave as women's cheeks.

Why did European women have higher and more prominent cheekbones than African women? Does this mean African women love their babies less? Not at all. Unfortunately, it was very hot in Africa, and the heat did not allow you to cuddle a baby for long before becoming hot and sweaty. It was uncomfortable for both mother and baby. After a short while, the mother had to put the baby down. Consequently, African women did not develop as high and fleshy cheekbones as European women. The cold climate in Europe allowed women to hug and cuddle a baby for a long time. It made both mother and baby warm and comfortable. This is why European women have developed higher and fuller cheekbones, whereas African women's cheekbones are less pronounced.

Why did Asian women have the least cheekbone development among the three groups of women? This characteristic resulted from the traditional Chinese hairstyle. Combing the hair back and pulling it tight and up at a $45°$ angle to make a knob on top of the head also pulled the skin at the corner of the eyes and restrained the skin below the eyes, preventing accumulation of fatty tissues in the cheekbone area. This is the reason northern Asian women

(Chinese, Korean, Japanese, and Mongolian) did not develop prominent and fleshy cheekbones like European women. However, you may notice that women in Southeast Asia have slightly higher and fleshier cheekbone. This is because their ancestors did not wear the traditional Chinese hairstyle.

You may have also noticed that many Asian people have less wrinkled skin on their foreheads and in the corners of their eyes. This makes Asian people look younger than their ages. Many people believe this may be attributed to their diets, lifestyles, or genetics. If it is genetic, then how did the gene develop? I believe that Asian people have fewer wrinkles again because of their traditional hairstyles, which pulled the skin on the forehead and in the corners of the eyes so tight that it prevented wrinkles from forming. Since this Chinese hairstyle continued for thousands of years, eventually, this trait became genetic among northern Asian people.

SUMMARY: The development of high, soft, fleshy cheekbones and concave cheeks among women was a result of motherhood. It was a modification of their cheeks and cheekbones to provide a better fit for the baby's head, so they could cuddle the baby longer. It became hereditary among women, and it is a trait of femininity. Since high cheekbones are not developed among young girls, it is also a trait of maturity, indicating that a woman is ready to be a mother. Men's cheekbones remained low and flat with less accumulation of fatty tissues, which also became a trait of masculinity.

Earlier, you may have doubted that the Chinese hairstyle caused slender eyes among many Asian people. By now, you should

62

be convinced that the influence of this thousand-year traditional hairstyle to Asians' facial development is not only limited to slender eyes but also to the development of small eyelids with little mobility, thin and loose eyebrows, and short eyelashes. It prevents the accumulation of fatty tissues over the cheekbone, leading to less pronounced cheeks among Asian women. It also explains why Asian people have fewer wrinkles on their foreheads and in the corners of their eyes, which make them looking younger.

2.11

FACE SHAPE

FACTS AND QUESTIONS: Face shape varies with age among individuals, and there are many shapes of the human face. You can find all face shapes in all groups of people. It is difficult to use facial shape alone to identify a person as to which group one may belong. However, there is a dominant face shape in each group of people. We can roughly divide people into two major groups based on a general observation of face shapes: European people as one group, and Asian and African people as the other.

Generally speaking, European people have long and narrow faces, which often are described as long oval- or oblong-shaped faces. Their heads are usually flat on both sides and their temples slight depressed, which make their faces even narrower and longer. They also seem to have longer noses, philtra, and chins than Asian and African people. Note: they may also have longer foreheads. We will not include the forehead because it may be magnified by a receding hairline. It is also true that Europeans' ears are more flattened to the side of head. It is uncommon for Europeans to have ears that stick out. Why do European people have narrower and longer faces, along with longer noses, philtra, and chins and flattened ears? Another interesting characteristic is the space between the eyes. Europeans' eyes are much closer to each other than Asian and African people's eyes. Why do European people have a narrower space between their eyes?

Asian and African people commonly have round-, square-, and oval-shaped faces. Both sides of their heads and temples slightly bulge out, which make their faces wider and shorter. They also have noticeably shorter noses, philtra, and chins. Their ears stick slightly outward. Why do Asians and African have more round and wider faces?

Another interesting characteristic is the lateral profile. When you look at European people's heads from the side, it is easily noticeable that they have a slightly convex face and a slightly convex profile at the back of the head. The lateral view of Asian and African people's heads shows a slightly flat face and a slightly flat profile at the back of the head. Since each group of people has a predominant face shape and head profile, it must be genetic. What created such genetic development?

MY THEORIES AND INTERPRETATIONS: I believe that different face shapes and head profiles were developed due to the climates people lived in. Because cold and hot climates caused people to sleep in certain positions, they directly affected the development of the face and head. Please remember that there were no air-conditioning or heating systems during the early days that allowed people to change the temperature inside their shelters. They had to find ways of sleeping to accommodate the temperature in which they lived.

In Europe, the climate was very cold. The temperature dropped even lower during the night. It was hard for people to stay warm while sleeping. To help with this, they likely wore their daytime clothing to bed and covered themselves with blankets or animal furs and skins. Still, it was not enough. Naturally, they curled their bodies while they were sleeping during the night. They put their arms in front of their chests and pulled both legs up to the abdominal area like a baby in the womb. This position helped them stay warm by trapping the heat in the chest and abdominal area. This is what we usually do when we feel cold at night. To have this kind body position, one must sleep sideways. When you sleep sideways, the side of your head rests on the pillow. It flattens the side of your head, depresses the temples, and flattens both ears to the side of the head. (You probably have noticed that a baby will have a flattened head on one side when a parent consistently puts the baby to sleep on the same side.) Since their faces couldn't grow sideways, they grew longer in length. As a result, their faces became narrower and longer, with both ears flattened to the side of the head. This is the reason very few Europeans have ears that stick outward and face front. At the same time, the forehead, nose, philtrum, and chin also grew proportionally longer. Their eyes also moved closer together. When you have a narrow face, your eyes cannot be located too far apart. This is why European people have narrow spaces between their eyes. To sleep constantly on the side of the head also caused a convex face shape and a convex profile at the back of the head. Over time, early humans in Europe gradually developed narrow and long face shapes, with both sides of the head flattened, depressed temples, a narrow space between the eyes, and flattened ears, which eventually became genetic among European people. This is why long oval- and oblong-shaped faces are most common among Europeans.

In Africa and southern Asia, the climate was hot. It was even hotter inside their shelters. This made sleep difficult for people. They needed to disperse their body heat. They couldn't sleep sideways with their bodies curled up like the Europeans did, as that would make them even hotter and sweatier. They needed to sleep facing up, with both arms spread to the side and away from the body and legs stretched straight and apart, so the body heat can disperse easily upward. This sleeping position helped them to cool the body, so they could sleep through the night. To sleep facing up, you must rest the back of the head on the pillow. In this position, you flattened the back of the head. It also caused to develop a flat face because gravity caused the face to develop sideways instead of upward. This is why Asians and Africans have slightly flat faces and flat at the back of the head in the lateral profile. At the same time, the head became wider on both sides. As a result, their faces looked shorter and rounder, with more space between the eyes and the ears slightly sticking outward. Proportionally, they also developed shorter foreheads, noses, philtra, and chins. Over time, African and Asian people developed wider faces with bulging temples and widely spaced eyes, which eventually became genetic among them. This is why round- and square-shaped faces are more dominant among Asian and African people. In the cooler climate in Asia, people developed oval-shaped faces due to sleeping in both sideways and facing up positions.

You can easily understand my theory by an experiment using Play-Doh. You make two models of the same human face with eyes, a nose, and a mouth. If you press on one head from both sides, then you will see the face becomes narrower and longer, the eyes move closer toward each other, and the nose and chin also become longer. This is exactly what happened to Europeans' faces, which was caused by sleeping on the side of the head. If you press down on the face of the other model from above, then the face becomes wider and rounder, and the eyes move away from each other. You also flatten the face and the back of the head. This resembles how the face shape of Asian and African people was developed—by sleeping facing up.

Some anthropologists believe that Europeans' eyes are located close to each other due to their hunting lifestyle. Moving the eyes closer in the front of the face helped them see the prey better. It is true that animals that are hunters in the wild have both eyes located in the front of the face, so they can concentrate their vision forward, whereas the eyes of grazing animals, such as antelopes and zebras, are usually located on the side of the head so they can see their predictors from all around. The downfall of this theory is that anthropologists couldn't explain why Asian and African people did not move their eyes closer. They were also hunters in the early days. In addition, this theory has a fundamental problem. Moving two eyes closer together does not help increase vision to hunt. As a matter of fact, it decreases your judgment of the distance in front of you. When your eyes are too close to each other, you will lose depth perception as if you have only one eye. We need two eyes located in the front, and we also need a certain space between the two eyes in order to gain a stereo view and determine the exact distance between two objects. If you look at the eyes of lions and tigers, the great hunters in the wild, their eyes are not close to each other. I believe that European people had developed narrower spaces between their eyes simply as a result of sleeping sideways. It is natural that your eyes would move closer together when your face became narrower. It has nothing to do with their hunting lifestyle.

SUMMARY: Although sleeping positions caused the development of different face shapes, the actual reason was attributed to different climates in different continents. The dominant narrow- and long-shaped face of European people was caused by sleeping sideways because of the extremely cold climate in Europe, whereas the dominant round-shaped face of Asian and African people was caused by sleeping facing up due to the hot climate. Both cases support my theory that climate has caused changes to human bodies. Some modifications are simply because of way of life and daily habit. In regard to the development of face shapes, changes occurred due to the way people slept. It was not an adaptation.

Regarding the development of the ears, many animals in the wild rely on their hearing to hunt or to hear their predators. Different animals have developed different ear shapes, such as long, round, big, small, facing front or to the side, or a wide angle of rotation. However, the development of humans' ears was quite different from animals in the wild. We do not use our hearing to hunt or to protect ourselves. Whether our ears are flattened to the sides of the head (like most Europeans) or sticking outward (like most Asians and Africans) was a result of our sleeping position, not because of offensive or defensive reasons.

2.12

SKIN COLOR

FACTS AND QUESTIONS: European people have light skin pigmentation and are commonly known as white people. Why do European people have white skin? African people have dark skin and are commonly known as black people. Why do African people have dark skin? Asian people have a great variation of skin color. Generally, northern Asians have light skin like the Europeans, whereas southern Asians have darker skin. Some people in eastern Indonesia and New Guinea are as dark as the African people. There is a decrease in skin pigmentation as we move away from the equatorial area. Why do people develop different skin pigmentations in different regions of the world?

It is common knowledge that our skin color has something to do with the amount of sunlight exposure. Most of us know that sunlight can change our skin color. But maybe it is the other way around: we change our skin color to adapt to different amounts of sunlight. So, is it the egg first or the chicken first? It is well-known that some Europeans can tan easily while others burn. Why? The truth is that the science of skin pigmentation goes much deeper than we know.

MY THEORIES AND INTERPRETATIONS: Scientists have found that our skin pigmentation is related to the amount of melanin we have under our skin. Melanin is a pigment substance that gives the skin its natural color, containing black eumelanin, brown eumelanin, and pheomelanin (pink color). It can slow down the penetration of UV radiation through our skin. It protects our bodies from intense sunlight. UV radiation can cause DNA damage to skin cells, leading to skin cancer and folate depletion (vitamin B complex occurs in leafy vegetables, essential for healthy eggs and human reproduction). Human bodies know how to produce the right amount of melanin to protect against different intensities of sunlight and UV radiation. This is why we have different skin pigmentation in different regions of the world.

In Africa, people in the equatorial area produce a high amount of melanin (predominantly black eumelanin) to protect themselves from intense sunlight and high levels of UV radiation. This is why African people have dark skin. In Europe, people are exposed to low levels of sunlight and radiation and so produce little black eumelanin, leading to light skin pigmentation. This is why Europeans have white skin. Therefore, dark skin is an adaptation to an environment with high UV radiation. This theory is strongly supported by the correlation of the distribution of skin color and the level of UV radiation around the world.

Although high UV radiation can damage our bodies, we do need a certain amount of UV radiation to help produce vitamin D, which helps the body absorb more calcium. It is essential for bone development and for the immune system and brain. Although UV light penetrates slowly through dark skin, dark-skinned people usually do not lack vitamin D while living in equatorial areas due to high levels of sunlight exposure.

However, in areas with low sunlight, dark-skinned people would not absorb sufficient UV radiation, resulting in vitamin D deficiency. This places them at higher risk of developing rickets, cancers, low immune system, and so on. When African people migrated to Europe forty-five thousand years ago, they faced the danger of vitamin D deficiency because of their dark skin. Consequently, a new theory postulates that early humans in Europe developed light skin to help produce enough vitamin D in an environment with low sunlight and UV radiation levels. Because light skin has very little melanin, allowing UV radiation to penetrate the skin much quicker, people don't need long exposure to sunlight to produce enough vitamin D. This is why European people have developed white skin. This theory became acceptable.

This theory is further enhanced by other study and research. Some scientists have noted that the low level of sunlight in Europe was due to a seasonal deficiency of sunlight. Others have used the Ozone Mapping Spectrometer data to measure UV radiation levels around the world, showing that more light-skinned people live in regions with low levels of UV radiation, such as in Europe. Hence, the theory that light skin was developed to adapt to the environment of low levels of sunlight and UV radiation to help increase production of vitamin D became overwhelmingly popular. (The preceding information is obtained from Wikipedia and other Internet sources.)

I disagree with this interpretation because I feel it has a fundamental problem. Early humans in Europe might not have had a problem of vitamin D deficiency as scientists believed. Inland hunters might have obtained sufficient vitamin D from eating reindeer meat and organs, which contained high amounts of vitamin D. Reindeer meat was the main food source of early humans in Europe (Dunbar and Waage, *Historical Geology*), whereas those who lived in the coastal areas of the Atlantic, Mediterranean, Black, and Caspian seas might also have obtained enough vitamin D from seafood. It shatters the theory that light skin was developed because of the need for vitamin D. If not, then what was the reason that European people developed white skin?

I believe that the light skin of European people was developed due to low levels of sunlight exposure and UV radiation but not because of a seasonal deficiency of sunlight or low levels of UV radiation in Europe. I believe that the light skin of early Europeans was developed as a result of living in their dark shelters (caves). To understand this, we must take ourselves back to the time forty-five thousand years ago in Europe. It was so cold that early humans had to stay inside their shelters behind closed doors (whatever they used to block the entrance) to prevent cold air from rushing in and to stop predators, resulting in a dark environment with little sunlight penetration. Because their skin had not been exposed to constant sunlight year-round, the melanin (predominantly black eumelanin), which was produced to protect the skin from sunlight and UV radiation, lost its purpose to serve the body. Their bodies started to produce lesser amounts of eumelanin in each generation. Without the presence of eumelanin in the upper skin, their skin became lighter in pigmentation, leading to white skin. In the wild, many species in dark caves have become colorless simply due to an absence of sunlight. Another reason for light skin development is attributed to the cold climate. Early humans in Europe wore thick clothing, presumably animal furs or skins. When they went outside, they bundled their bodies from head to toe. Their thick clothing prevented penetration of sunlight and UV radiation. No matter how bright or how high UV radiation from snow reflection might be, their bodies were never exposed to it except for their faces, and they stayed outside for only a short time. This was the reason they had low sunlight exposure and low levels of UV radiation, leading to low production of melanin and light skin. It is common knowledge that clothing can protect our skin from sunlight and UV radiation. Many people have tanned faces and arms but still maintain light skin under their shirts. This phenomenon supports the theory that the light skin color of early European people was developed in part due to wearing thick clothing year-round. Over time, white skin became genetic among early humans in Europe. It has noting to do with the need for vitamin D.

It is reasonable to conclude that vitamin D deficiency was not the initial reason to trigger the development of light skin. However, the need for vitamin D might have increased during the time after the Ice Age when European people did not rely on reindeer meat for food, and there were no other supplements. This was lucky for European people. Their light skin helped them produce enough vitamin D in an environment with low levels of sun exposure. However, light skin also brought them some health disadvantages. In a sunny environment, they are more susceptible to sunburn, skin cancer, and folate depletion because UV radiation penetrates the light skin quickly without melanin blocking it.

Why do some Europeans tan easily and perfectly and others burn? Melanin is produced in the lowest level of the epidermis. When we are exposed to intense sunlight, melanin moves to the upper level of the skin to protect us from UV radiation because melanin can dissipate UV radiation (Internet information). When the sunlight becomes more intense, your body moves more melanin to the upper level. Consequently, your skin becomes darker. Since most Europeans have more brown eumelanin and less black eumelanin, it produces a brownish-tan. During times of low sunlight exposure, the melanin migrates back to the lower epidermis. As a result, the tan fades, and you become light skinned again. This is why some Europeans can get a tan in only a week when they go sunbathing and then return to light skin in a month or so when they are not exposed to sunlight. This is similar to a country that has an army located in the interior as a reserve (assuming the body is the country and melanin is the army). When there is an enemy invasion at the border, the army moves to the front line to protect against the invasion. As the enemy's invasion increases, more soldiers are moved to the front line. When the war ends, the army moves back to the interior and reduces in size. This privilege only applies to Europeans whose early ancestors had experience with exposure to seasonal, intense sunlight. For example: those people who lived in southern Europe by the Mediterranean Sea had more experience with sunbathing. They have plenty of melanin in the lower epidermis as a reserve and are able to produce more. In other words, their melanin is always ready to move to the front line.

Those Europeans whose ancestors lived in much colder areas of Europe have never had experience with sunbathing; thus, they had very little amounts of black eumelanin, or none, in the lower epidermis and had no ability to produce more. It had become part of their genetic package. Therefore, when their descendants go sunbathing, their bodies don't have enough melanin to move up to protect their skin. Without black eumelanin in the upper epidermis, their skin stays white. Without sufficient melanin to protect the skin from UV radiation, they get sunburned. To go back to our earlier analogy, a country without an army in reserve cannot defend its border. This is genetic, and there is not much help for it. Although they didn't get the tan they wished for, most of them have inherited a pair of blue or green eyes.

Why did some European have freckles? When some Europeans are exposed to sunlight, their bodies realize they need to protect their skin from UV radiation. Unfortunately, they don't have any black eumelanin that they can use. Instead, their bodies use the pheomelanin (another type of melanin in the human body) to protect their skin. Pheomelanin contains pigments of pink to red hues, but it is usually not enough to cover the entire body. As a result, it distributes unevenly and forms freckles. Areas that are exposed to more sunlight, such as noses, shoulders, and lower arms, develop more freckles.

In Asia, there are variations of skin pigmentation in different regions. Generally, people in the equatorial area have dark skin, which gradually changes to lighter skin northward as you move farther away from the equator. This is mainly because the sun is more intense and has higher radiation levels in the equatorial area. Skin pigmentation is also highly correlated with the amount of clothing people wear during the year. The reason is that thick clothing blocks the sunlight and reduces the intensity and radiation. As a result, their melanin stays in the lower epidermis, leading to lighter pigmentation in the surface skin. Therefore, northern Asian people who wear more clothing and for longer periods of time during the year have lighter skin. Southern Asians who wear less clothing and often bare their bodies usually have dark skin. The only exception is the Eskimo people who live in the Arctic region of North America. They wear thick clothing year-round and still maintain their brown faces. This is attributed to high UV radiation from snow reflection and to living in bright igloos made of snow blocks.

Besides protecting our bodies from UV radiation damage, melanin also helps to increase sexual attraction and appearance by concentrating melanin in certain parts of the human body. It produces different shades of pink, red, brown, or nearly black in lips, nipples, areolae, penises, labia, and vaginas. This was originally developed to attract mates to increase human reproduction. Explanation: all living organisms have two main goals—survival and reproduction. Survival involves food and adaptation, whereas reproduction determines the continuation of a species. When a living organism cannot find food or is unable to adapt to the environment, it will die. If a species cannot reproduce, then it will face extinction. Sexual attraction becomes important in the process of reproduction. Human beings are no exception. This is why men want to be strong and handsome, and women want to make themselves more beautiful and attractive. Long before humans invented makeup, our early ancestors provided certain parts of our bodies with higher levels of pigmentation to increase sexual attraction and appearance in order to attract mates and to assure humans have descendants. Consequently, the attractive color of our sexual organs and lips became genetic among different groups of people.

SUMMARY: There are many theories and hypotheses about skin pigmentation. Some theories have been proven wrong and downplayed. Others have been enhanced by subsequent research and become more acceptable and popular. The recent theory that light skin was developed to adapt to low levels of UV radiation to help the production of vitamin D is most popular, but just because it is popular does not mean it is right. I, on the other hand, believe that the light skin of European people was developed initially due to prolonged living in dark shelters and to wearing thick clothing year-round. Light skin might have helped Europeans to produce vitamin D after the Ice Age, but it was not the initial reason that triggered the development of light skin.

2.13

BODY HAIR AND BEARDS

FACTS AND QUESTIONS: Europeans have more body hair than Asian and African people. European men also have big mustaches and bushy beards. Why do they have more body hair and bushy beards? Why do Asians and Africans have sparse body hair? Were early humans hairy, or did they have less hair?

MY THEORIES AND INTERPRETATIONS: Scientists believe that the primate ancestors of human and chimpanzee lineages diverged about seven million years ago. At that time, the ancestors of early humans had light skin and a hairy body like the chimpanzees. About 4.5 to 2 million years ago, they moved out of rain forests to the savannas of East Africa. The heat in the savannas was too hot for their hairy bodies. They had to lose their body hair (fur) to help with cooling because fur trapped body heat and prevented the evaporation of sweat. They also developed more sweat glands to increase the dissipation of body heat. These adaptations helped them to hunt for longer times under the sun. As they lost their body hair, their white skin became vulnerable to damage by UV radiation from the sun. Their skin started changing to a darker color under the sun, which was another important evolutionary adaptation because the darker skin color protected them from intense sunlight. (The preceding information was collected from Wikipedia.)

I believe that the primate ancestors of early humans did not move out of the rain forest voluntary. Because the rain forest provided them with food and shade from the hot equatorial sun, they would have preferred to stay in an environment where they were familiar and comfortable. They would not leave their normal habitat for a new and unfavorable environment unless they were forced to. I believe they were likely driven out of the rain forest by chimpanzees because of food competition due to a growing population. Chimpanzees, then, were probably stronger and bigger than the primate ancestors of early humans. Our early ancestors had no choice but to abandon their normal habitat and migrate to an unknown environment. Savannas were hot, without much shade, and it was harder to find food. To survive, they had to make changes to adapt to their new environment. Adaptation promotes the evolution of a species. They began to lose their body hair and develop more sweat glands to help with cooling; they developed darker skin to protect from UV radiation; they stood more upright to help with walking; they developed longer legs for traveling longer distances; their feet and hands changed to adapt to terrestrial life; they learned to hunt in a savanna instead of relying on fruits; and they gradually changed from gatherers to hunters. As a result, they became a more efficient and stronger species. After millions of years of evolution, ancestors of the modern human, *Homo sapiens*, emerged in Africa, whereas the chimpanzees stayed as chimpanzees without much change because they still lived in tropical rain forests in the same habitat as millions of years ago.

I predict that early humans had dark skin with sparse body hair (visible hair) when they emerged in southwestern Ethiopia. The only dense hair that remained was likely on the head, in the armpits, and around the sex organs, which were maintained for reasons of sexual attraction and privacy. Losing body hair or fur might not need a long time to occur. Some species in the wild can shed their winter fur in a few weeks to adapt to the summer heat. However, it might have taken thousands of years for sparse body hair to become genetic. The primate ancestors of early humans spent millions of years in the savannas of Africa. When early humans emerged, they spent another hundred thousand years along the Nile River. By the time they left Africa and migrated to Asia, they had sparse body hair, which likely had already become a genetic trait. This is why Asian and African people have very little body hair.

When early humans migrated to Europe, they had dark skin with sparse body hair. The climate in Europe was so cold that they had to cover their bodies with animal furs and skins, but that was not enough. Their hairless bodies lost body heat quickly and couldn't stand the cold. To help their bodies stay warmer, they started to grow more body hair. The increase in body hair was obviously to adapt to the cold climate in Europe, which eventually became a genetic trait among European people. This is why European people have more body hair than Asians and Africans.

Why do most European men have big mustaches and bushy beards? I believe that their mustaches and beards were developed to keep their lips, faces, and chins warm. In subzero temperatures and blizzard conditions, the human face could easily become frozen and susceptible to frostbite. They could cover their heads and bodies with animal furs and skins but not the face because they needed to see and to breathe. Big mustaches and bushy beards were grown to adapt to the cold weather, so they could gather more food and hunt for longer times outside. Over time, big mustaches and bushy beards became genetic among European men. Women stayed in their shelters, taking care of the children and conducting inside work; thus, they had less exposure to the extreme weather outside. Therefore, there was no need to grow hair (mustaches or beards) to keep their faces warm. This is why European women maintained hairless faces, whereas men's mustaches and beards became a trait of masculinity. Light-colored mustaches and beards are characteristics of Europeans, which distinguish them from other groups of people. (The development of light-colored hair is described in section 2.15—HAIR COLOR.)

SUMMARY: In geological history, there were numerous records of constant environmental changes, such as global climate, sea level, distribution of land and ocean, mountain building, topography and landscape, vegetation, food sources, predictors, diseases, and so on. All these changes affect the habitat and survival of all living organisms. As a result, all species face changes and must be able to adapt to the new environment. Fortunately, most of these changes are slow and gradual, except for catastrophe, such as volcanic explosions, earthquakes, tsunami, and meteorites. Most species would have time to evolve or to migrate to another environment.

In the event of a major change of environment, all living organisms have three choices.

1. They change their bodies and their lifestyles to adapt to the new environment. Those species that are able to adapt usually survive and flourish.
2. Organisms that are not able to adapt to the new environment migrate to another environment that is more suitable for them. Some of them even change from terrestrial to aquatic life or vice versa. They also survive and sometimes thrive.
3. Those species that do not want to change or move away usually decline and become extinct.

Whatever the changes may be, all living species always have these three choices—adapt, move, or decline. Human beings are no exception. We also have to face changing environments, and we also have these three choices. In addition, we are living in a world of competition. Competition can inspire people to achieve a higher level and to discover the best of humanity. When we look back to the early history of primates, they would not have evolved to a higher species if they didn't strive to survive and to compete for a better life.

2.14

HAIR TEXTURE

FACT AND QUESTIONS: We know that Asian people have straight hair; European people have wavy hair; and African people have curly, spiral, and coiled hair. A half-century ago, scientists knew that Asians' straight hair shafts are round in a cross section, Europeans' wavy hair is oval, and the Africans' curly and spiral hair is a lenticular or tubular shape. Why have these three groups of people developed different types of hair in different continents?

Hair density decreases as we age. On average, European people have significantly more hair than African people. European blonds have about one hundred and forty thousand hair strands, whereas African people have about one hundred thousand. Asians are in between one hundred thousand and one hundred and forty thousand. They also have thicker and stronger hair shafts. Why do people in different continents have different amounts of hair? Another interesting fact is that red-haired people have only ninety thousand strands, the lowest among Europeans.

Curly, spiral, and kinky hair are unique to African people. They distinguish them from other groups of people. Some scientists have thought that Africans' curly and spiral hair might be due to hot climates and developed to protect them from UV radiation, but they couldn't explain how they were developed. If this theory stands, then the curly nature of hair should decrease as we move away from the equator. In other words, Asian people who live in the Tropic of Cancer area should have wavy hair, and European people who live far away from the equator should have straight hair. Unfortunately, the curliness of human hair does not coincide with the distance from the equator. Asian people have straight instead of wavy hair, whereas European people have wavy instead of straight hair. Furthermore, if Africans' hair developed to protect them from UV radiation, then they should have grown more hair to block the radiation. Contrarily, they have the least amount of hair among the three groups of people. Besides, African people have dark skin to protect them from UV radiation, so why would they need additional protection? There are many other theories regarding the curl patterns of hair. Today, scientists still have not come up with a satisfactory theory that can explain the development of hair texture among these three groups of people. As stated in Wikipedia: the derivations of hair texture are not fully understood. In other words, no one knows how hair textures developed before they became genetic traits.

The questions that wait to be answered are: Why do African people have curly and spiral hair and have the least amount of hair? Why do Asian people have straight hair with a round hair shaft? Why is their hair thicker and stronger? Why do European people have wavy hair and the highest density of hair?

MY THEORIES AND INTERPRETATIONS: To understand the development of hair texture, I will take you back to the beginning when early humans emerged in East Africa. As described in section 2.13—BODY HAIR AND BEARDS, early humans' primate ancestors lost their body hair to help cool their bodies when they migrated to the hot savanna. They also developed dark skin to protect them from UV radiation damage. When early humans emerged, they had shed more hair on the head to create space for more sweat glands, which helped to dissipate heat by sweating. Less hair also made evaporation easier. This made them more efficient to adapt to the hot sun in Africa because the human brain could easily get sunstroke when overheated. This is why African people have the least amount of hair among the three groups of people.

Less hair on the head, however, made their head more exposed to intense sunlight. The human body recognized the danger of an overheated brain. I believe that early humans in Africa developed a tubular hair shaft instead of a round one to reduce the occurrence of sunstroke. The reason is that tubular hair shafts gave more shade than round shafts. Even though they had less hair, their tubular hair shaft still gave full shade coverage over their head. Therefore, their scalp would not be exposed to intense sunlight and UV radiation, and it provided the additional benefit of having more space for more sweat glands to help with cooling. Therefore, the tubular hair shaft of the African people was developed to adapt to the hot sun in Africa. This was a remarkable design of the human body among the African people. Note: UV radiation might not have been an important issue to African people because they had already developed dark skin to protect against UV radiation.

How did African people develop curly and spiral hair? The curly and spiral nature of Africans' hair developed naturally because of the tubular hair shaft. Explanation: Tubular hair shafts usually have uneven growth on each side. When one side grows faster than the other, the hair starts to curl (the side with faster growth will curl over the side with slower growth). The two ends (cross-section view) of a tubular hair shaft also have different growth rates. When one end grows faster than the other end, it will produce spiral or kinky hair. In other words, the curly, spiral, and kinky nature of Africans' hair is attributed to the differential growth of the tubular hair shafts. The curly nature of Africans' hair offered additional shade coverage for their heads (a spiral hair shaft provides more shadow than a straight hair shaft). Along with these benefits, their hair also served as insulation against the hot sun. Spiral and kinky hairs tend to get tangled with one another to form a nest-like structure, which traps a layer of cooler air. There is no doubt that the curly and kinky tubular hair shaft of African people was developed to adapt to the intense sunlight and to prevent UV radiation damage so they could survive in Africa. Over time, this type of hair texture became genetic among African people. Their descendants inherit the same hair texture no matter where they are born.

Early humans in Africa might have already used stones with sharp edges to cut their hair short. It would be unbearably hot and sweaty if their curly hair covered their necks and shoulders. When they cut their hair short, it made their hair more curly. When they migrated to Europe about forty-five thousand years ago, they had dark skin with short curly and kinky hair. The cold weather in Europe was something they had never experienced. They needed to cover not only their bodies with animal furs and skins but also their necks. Naturally, they let their hair grow longer to help keep their necks and shoulders warm. As their hair grew longer and hung down, each hair strand carried more weight. The weight pulled the shaft of each hair longer and straighter. Gradually, their spiral and curly hair became wavy. At the same time, the original tubular hair shaft gradually changed to oval. Explanation: When you pull a spiral or coiled rope consistently, it will gradually become less spiral and coiled. When you release the rope after a certain time, the rope will stay wavy instead of returning to its original spiral form. The circumference of the rope (cross-section view) also changes from irregular to oval. This is why European people have wavy hair with an oval shaft.

Oval hair also has a different growth rate around the circumference, but not as much as tubular hair. The shape of the hair shaft determines the degree of waviness. The shape of the hair shaft can be changed depending on the hair's length and weight. Short hair has less weight to pull each strand, resulting in a lenticular oval shaft, which produces curly and wavy hair. Long hair has a heavier weight to pull each strand, resulting in an oval or round shaft, which produces less wavy hair. Those people whose ancestors lived in colder areas or have customs of growing longer hair are likely to have less wavy hair. Those people whose ancestors lived in warmer areas or wore their hair in shorter lengths are likely to have more wavy hair. Therefore, there are variations of hair textures and degrees of waviness among Europeans.

Human brains are very sensitive to different climates. If it is too hot, then you get heatstroke. If it is too cold, then you suffer from hypothermia. In a cold climate, it is very important to keep the head warm. Human bodies know this well. How did early humans in Europe keep their heads warm before they had developed the hat? Naturally, early humans in Europe gradually increased the amount of hair on their heads and bodies and grew bigger mustaches and beards. This is why European people are more hairy than Asians and Africans. The high density of hair among European people was developed to adapt to the cold weather in Europe. This is why blond people have one hundred and forty thousand hair strands, more than any other groups of people. Together with the wavy texture, it became genetic among European people. Red-haired people have only ninety thousand strands, but they have thicker hair shafts that have helped to keep their heads warm.

About seventy thousand years ago, when early humans left Africa and migrated east to Asia, they experienced a seasonal and mild climate for the first time. They let their short curly and coiled hair grow longer. It was not too hot to have long hair, which helped to keep their necks warm in the wintertime and increased their attraction and identity. As described earlier, longer hair placed greater weight on the spiral hair, which gradually became wavy. The hair shaft gradually changed from tubular to lenticular, from lenticular to oval. It is believed that early Asians might have had wavy hair for thousands of years. It wasn't until the dawn of civilization that early humans in northern China started to pay attention to their appearance, dressed well, and combed their hair. The Chinese combed their hair back and pulled it tight to make a knob on top of their heads, or they wore their hair in long ponytails or braids. All these hairstyles required pulling the hair tight, which gradually caused their wavy hair to become straight. Explanation: when you constantly pull wavy strands tight, they will eventually become straight. Long ponytails and braids are heavy in weight, pulling the hair strands all day long. Over time, the Chinese hairstyle changed their hair shafts from an oval shape to a round shape. A round hair shaft grows evenly all around, which caused the hair to grow straight. On top of that, hair shafts also grew thicker and stronger to resist the pulling caused by the weight of long hair. Of course, Chinese culture influenced the surrounding countries and their people, who also wore the same Chinese hairstyle. Consequently, most Asian people (Chinese, Koreans, Japanese, and Mongolians) have straight, thick, and strong hair with round shafts, which became genetic traits among them. The exception is people in Southeast Asia who still have slightly wavy hair because they were not influenced by Chinese culture.

SUMMARY: African people's spiral and coiled hair with its tubular hair shaft was developed to adapt to an environment of hot and intense sunlight. European people's wavy hair resulted from growing longer hair to keep their necks and shoulders warm in a cold climate. Their original curly hair became wavy due to the weight of their longer hair. Asian people's straight hair resulted from the weight of long hair, together with the constant pulling and combing associated with the traditional Chinese hairstyle. It caused the spiral hair to become straighter, thicker, and stronger. At the same time, the original tubular hair shaft gradually changed to oval and finally became round. The different hair textures of these three groups of people were caused by different reasons. No wonder scientists have difficulty finding a single theory that could explain and link the development of different hair textures.

The density of hair of African, Asian, and European people correlates with the climate of each continent. In the hot equatorial area, people have less hair to help with cooling. As you move farther away from the equator, people need more hair to keep their heads warm. European people have the highest density of hair because they lived in the coldest continent. In the wild, it is common that many animals grow thicker hair or fur to keep their bodies warm during the wintertime, such as caribou, bison, and mountain sheep.

2.15

HAIR COLOR

FACTS AND QUESTIONS: Most Asian and African people have black hair, except for older people who have gray or white hair. Why do Asians and Africans have black hair? Light hair colors are characteristics of European people, which occur in the hair on their heads as well as in their eyebrows, mustaches, beards, and body hair. What are the causes of light hair? Blond and red hair is exclusive to people of European origin. There is a great variation of hair color among Europeans, such as light blond to dark blond, light red to dark red, light brown to dark brown, and black or a mixture of these colors. Why do European people have such a diversity of hair color? Why is blond hair more common among children than adults?

According to the distribution maps of light hair and light eyes in and near Europe ("Why do Europeans have so many hair and eye colors?" Peter Frost), light-haired people are most common in the Baltic Sea countries (situated in northwestern Europe), such as Norway, Sweden, and Finland. They account for 80 percent or more of the population. In the surrounding countries, including western Russia, Netherlands, and Great Britain, 50 to 79 percent of people have light-colored hair. The occurrence decreases outward toward the south and east. The distribution of light hair correlates with the distribution of blue and green eyes, which also have the highest concentration in the Baltic Sea area. Why did the distribution of light hair correlate with the distribution of blue and green eyes?

There are many studies and publications of hair color available on the Internet. The knowledge of human hair color is vast and complicated. To summarize, we human beings have a certain amount of melanin (pigment) in our bodies. Melanin is produced by melanocytes in the basal layer of the epidermis. Its main purpose is to protect our skin from UV radiation damage. Melanin is also found in our hair, which determines our hair color.

The two types of melanin that control our hair color are eumelanin and pheomelanin. Basic hair pigmentation is determined by the following:

1. Black eumelanin: A high amount of black eumelanin causes black hair, whereas low amounts result in gray hair.
2. Brown eumelanin: A high amount of brown eumelanin causes brown hair, whereas a small amount results in blond hair when there are no other pigments.
3. Pheomelanin: Pheomelanin contains hues of pink, orange, and red. High concentrations of pheomelanin with a small amount of brown eumelanin produce red hair. The highest concentration of naturally red-haired people are found in Ireland and Scotland (more than 10 percent) and in the Kazan region of Russia. This number decreases to about 5 percent in Norway, Sweden, and Netherlands and declines southward toward the Mediterranean Sea.

Our hair color is not determined by one single pigment, but rather by a combination of different pigments in different proportions. Furthermore, mixed marriages in which the parents have different hair colors produce more diversity of hair color. Melanin also changes in its amount as we age, resulting in gray and white hair. This is why there is a wide range of human hair color. The genetics of hair color are not fully understood. Some scientists believe that at least two gene pairs control hair color. However, it still does not account for all the different shades of human hair colors. Note: the above information is collected from Wikipedia and other Internet sources.

We know that different types of melanin caused human hair pigmentations. We also know what type of melanin produces what kind of hair color. The questions here are: Why did the light hair color predominantly occur among European people? How did light hair develop before it became genetic? Why did it occur more in the Baltic Sea region and decrease southward toward the Mediterranean Sea? Why didn't some light-skinned (white-skinned) Asians develop blond hair?

MY THEORIES AND INTERPRETATIONS: In Africa and Asia, early humans produced predominantly black eumelanin to protect their skin from UV radiation damage. As black eumelanin migrated to the upper epidermis, their skin became darker pigmentation. At the same time, their hair also shared an abundance of black eumelanin, which produced black hair. This became genetic among Africans and Asians. This is why African and most southeast Asian people have dark skin and black hair. Many northern Asian people have fair skin pigmentation. Their white skin was not genetic. It resulted from low levels of sunlight exposure due to wearing thick clothing in a colder climate. (See section 2.12—SKIN COLOR for more details.) They actually have abundant black eumelanin in the lower epidermis, which has not migrated to the upper epidermis due to the absence of sunlight. This is why they have white skin and still have black hair.

When early humans migrated to Europe from Africa forty-five thousand years ago, they had dark skin with black hair. They had plenty of black eumelanin like their African ancestors. During those days, Europe was so cold that most of them had to stay inside their dark caverns, wearing thick animal furs and skins. Since their skin had very little exposure to sunlight, they had no need for black eumelanin to protect them from UV radiation. This environment of low sunlight exposure continued for a long time. Gradually, their bodies produced less and less black eumelanin. Consequently, their skin developed a light pigmentation.

Along with the decrease of black eumelanin production, the brown eumelanin and pheomelanin became more dominant. Explanation: we all have some brown eumelanin and pheomelanin in our bodies. When black eumelanin is abundant, other pigments are subdued. Just like when we paint a picture, the color black can cover all other colors. When there is a lesser amount of black, light colors become more pronounced. Consequently, brown eumelanin produced brown hair among Europeans, small amounts of brown eumelanin without the presence of other pigments produced blond hair, and pheomelanin produced red hair. Eventually, light hair became genetic among European people. After thousands of years of intermarriages among people from different regions of Europe, their descendants produced a wide diversity of hair colors.

Many European babies and young children have blond hair, which indicates that their early ancestors were blond. Blond hair was produced due to a low amount of brown eumelanin without other pigments. As they grow older, they are exposed to more sunlight and start to produce more eumelanin, either black or brown, to protect their skin. As a result, their hair changes to brown when brown eumelanin increases, and it changes to darker hair when black eumelanin increases. This is why there are fewer adults who have true blond hair. Explanation: European people gradually abandoned their dark cave dwellings after the Ice Age. They were exposed to more outdoor living and sunlight as the climate became warmer. Modern globalization brought them to different regions of the world and exposed them to higher levels of sunlight. Consequently, modern European adults have changed to darker hair along with the increase of eumelanin.

Living in dark shelters (caverns) caused the decrease of black eumelanin production among early humans in Europe. The amount of time they had to stay inside their shelters depended on the climate in that region. In a very cold region, such as northern Europe and the Baltic Sea area, people had to stay inside their shelters for a longer time. Consequently, they produced very little black eumelanin, or none, which led to more blond- and red-haired people. In warmer climates, such as in the Mediterranean Sea area, people spent less time inside their shelters and had more sun exposure. As a result, they had various amounts of black and brown eumelanin in their bodies, which resulted in more brown- and darker-hair people with less blond- and red-haired population.

The distribution of light-haired populations correlates with the distribution of blue- and green-eyed populations. Both appear with a higher frequency in the Baltic Sea area and decrease toward the Mediterranean Sea. As previously described in section 2.4—EYE COLOR, blue and green eyes were developed to enhance their vision in their dark shelters. They also developed light hair due to a lower production of black eumelanin attributed to low levels of sunlight exposure. All these traits were developed due to prolonged and continuous living in dark shelters because of an extremely cold climate. The colder the area it was, the more time people spent inside their dark shelters. If my theory stands, then the Baltic Sea region had to be the coldest area in Europe forty-five thousand years ago. This theory is confirmed by the distribution of the ice sheet in the Northern Hemisphere during the Ice Age (Dunbar and Waage, *Historical Geology*). It shows the center of the ice field in Europe was located in the Baltic Sea region. This is why Baltic Sea countries have the highest concentration of light-haired people and blue- and green-eyed populations, which then decreases outward toward the Mediterranean Sea as the climate warms.

SUMMARY: A hypothesis by Peter Frost states that the high concentration of blond people in the Baltic Sea region might be due to sexual selection because men like blond-haired women more. Since the Baltic Sea region was totally covered by ice sheets during the Ice Age, early people relied on hunting because there were no fruits to gather. Men likely lived shorter lives because of the harsh conditions related to chasing the herd in the snow, or they may have died in a blizzard. There were fewer men than women. Since women relied on men for food, it was necessary for women to compete for men. Blond hair and blue and green eyes were developed to attract men. This is why there were high concentrations of light-haired and light-eyed people in the Baltic Sea region. Note: it is true that male animals and insects in the wild develop bright colors to attract mates. In this case, the female developed light hair to attract the male.

Peter Frost presents distribution maps related to the light-haired and light-eyed populations to support his hypothesis. His maps are a valuable contribution to the study of anthropology. However, his hypothesis does not explain why Asian and African women did not develop blond hair and blue or green eyes to attract men. Women (in all regions) had been relying on men for food and survival for tens of thousands of years before modernization. You would think that all women should have developed brightly colored features to attract men, not just European women. There is another weak spot of Frost's hypothesis: most people are attracted to something they don't have. In regard to sexual attraction, a blond man may not be particularly interested in a blond woman because he himself has blond hair. He likely is more interested in dark hair. This is true for some thin men who prefer heavy women. Furthermore, it is very likely that there were no marriage laws to restrict one man from having more than one wife during humans' early days. When there were more women than men, stronger men would simply take more women. There was no need for women to develop special features to attract men. Therefore, Frost's hypothesis of sexual selection may not be the right reason to cause high concentrations of light-haired and light-eyed people in the Baltic Sea region.

I believe that both traits of light hair and blue and green eyes were initially developed due to prolonged and continuous living in dark shelters due to the extremely cold weather in the Baltic Sea region, not because of sexual selection. Early humans had decreased the production of black eumelanin due to low sunlight exposure in their dark shelters, which made the light pigments more dominant, leading to the emergence of light skin and hair. Contemporaneously, the dark environment inside their shelters caused them to develop blue and green eyes to enhance their vision. (See section 2.4—EYE COLOR for more details.) Since the Baltic Sea region was the coldest area in Europe, people had to stay in their dark shelters for longer periods of time, which caused most of them to develop light hair and light-colored eyes. Their reproduction led to higher concentrations and more diversity of light hair and light eye colors in that region.

My theory is fully supported by the geographic distribution of light hair and blue-and green-eyed people, which is highly correlated with the distribution of ice fields in Europe during the Ice Age. All these traits decrease their frequency as we moved away from the center of the ice fields, which were situated in the Baltic Sea region. Away from the region, the climate became warmer. People did not have to stay in their dark shelters as long. Consequently, light-haired and blue- and green-eyed populations decreased, along with the increase of darker hair and darker eyes people.

2.16

BALDNESS

FACTS AND QUESTIONS: Baldness is something we want to know more about because many of us, particularly men, worry about it. Among European people, around 30 percent of men start losing their hair in a great amount in their thirties. About 50 percent of men in Norway have noticeable baldness by age fifty. Baldness affects forty million people in the United States. However, baldness is much less common among Asian and African people. Only one out of four Chinese men have started balding by age fifty (Wikipedia and other Internet sources). Why does baldness occur more among European men than among Asians and Africans? Why is baldness particularly common among Norwegian people?

Another interesting fact is the pattern of baldness. Most common baldness starts in the hairline above the forehead, which is known as a receding hairline. It starts from the lateral sides above the forehead and then progresses toward the top of head in an M shape along the hairline. Another common place of baldness is on the top of the head (the crown). These types of baldness are most common among males and are known as male pattern baldness. Why do men have these baldness patterns? Unless one goes totally bald, baldness does not occur on the lateral sides or the lower back side of the head. It is almost unheard of anyone growing bald on the lower side of the head and still having hair on top of the head. Why? Women do experience hair thinning at an older age, but it is uncommon for women to go bald at a young age as men do. Why are there fewer occurrences of baldness among women than men?

Baldness includes two main types of hair loss. One is overall hair thinning due to aging. This occurs among older people and is part of the course of life. This is similar to having wrinkles in that we all have more wrinkles as we age. The other baldness type commonly occurs among men who have started losing their hair before old age. Scientists still have not found answers as to why people start losing their hair in their thirties, while they are still totally healthy.

Although baldness may be caused by many factors, such as aging, hormones, nutrition, diseases, and infections, common baldness is believed to be hereditary and genetic. How did the gene develop? Another interesting puzzle is why do bald men still have full bushy beards and big mustaches? You would think that if a man lost the hair on the head, then he should also lose the beard and mustache as well. As we all know, the genetic history of baldness is not fully understood.

MY THEORIES AND INTERPRETATIONS: I believe that the gene of baldness among Europeans was developed as a result of wearing hats in the cold climate. To understand my theory, we must go back to a time when early humans migrated to Europe forty-five thousand years ago from Africa. They had black and curly hair with about one hundred thousand hair strands (assuming they had about the same hair strands as present-day African people). During the Ice Age, they had to wear animal furs and skins to protect their bodies from the cold climate. They let their hair grow longer to keep their necks and shoulders warm. They also increased the amount of hair to about one hundred and forty thousand strands to help keep their heads warm. The increase of hair strands was developed to adapt to the cold weather in Europe. (See section 2.14—HAIR TEXTURE for more details.)

During early settlement time, most of northern Europe was covered with snow and ice sheets. Part of the year, the temperature was probably like today's Antarctica. Just having more hair on top of the head was not enough for early humans to keep their heads warm, especially men who had to stay outside to hunt. To chase the herds of reindeer in the snow and blizzards, you can be sure that they had to cover their heads with something, most likely animal fur. Whatever they used would be the earliest invention of the hat.

Without doubt, early European men wore hats when they were outside in the cold. Hair was grown to protect our head from either hot sun or cold temperatures. In cold climates, the main purpose of hair is to keep the head warm. That was why early humans had grown more hair after they had settled in Europe. When people wore hats, they greatly helped to trap the heat and kept the head warmer than hair. Their hair had lost the purpose of serving the head. Hair in the area covered by the hat started to shed. As the saying goes, "If you don't use it, you lose it."

To understand why baldness occurs only above the forehead and on top of the head, we must first understand how hats were made and worn. Today, hats are worn for different reasons and occasions. However, early humans in Europe wore hats for one reason: to keep their heads warm. Therefore, the common area covered by the hat was the top of the head and the forehead. This was because hats must be the right size to be useful and comfortable. If they covered only a small part of the head, then the wind would blow them away. If they covered the entire head, ears, and neck, although it might be very useful in extremely cold weather, then it would reduce hearing and could become too hot in different weather conditions. The most useful hats in early days were those that covered the upper half of the head, including the forehead, top, and upper portion of the back of the head. This type of hat stayed tight on the head and kept the most important part of the head warm. The forehead was the first place that got cold when facing cold wind. Therefore, most people pulled their hats lower to cover their foreheads to keep them warm. Sometimes, the front fringe of a hat also helped to block bright sunlight and to reduce blurred vision caused by snow reflection. No matter the type of hat or how people wore them, their foreheads and the tops of their heads were always covered. As a result, the hairline above the forehead and the top area of the head started to lose hair because hair in those areas was no longer needed to keep the head warm. With less hair on the head, their heads became more vulnerable to cold, and they had a greater need to wear hats. The more they wore hats, the more hair they shed. This was how baldness developed in the front hairline above the forehead and on the top of the head. Since early men in Europe relied on hunting for food, they all had to wear hats during hunting trips. Consequently, most men lost their hair in the area covered by the hats. Over time, baldness became genetic among European men.

What caused M-pattern baldness above the forehead? The most common baldness among men involves losing the hair on the lateral sides above the forehead, with some hair remaining in the middle, forming an M-shaped hairline. This M-shaped baldness developed originally as a result of selective hair loss. Hair loss did not occur simultaneously and evenly in the area covered by the hat. The hair that was less useful would be shed first, such as in the lateral sides above the forehead. The hair in the middle might be still needed on the days when people did not wear hats because they still helped to keep the forehead warm. This is why that hair was retained to be shed later. It is similar to a company that decides to reduce its staff. Workers who are less needed will be let go first. Workers who are still making money for the company will be retained. This is why a receding hairline occurs in an M shape, progressing toward the top of the head. This M-shaped receding hairline also became a genetic trait of baldness.

Most hats did not cover the lateral side and the lower back side of the head for practical reasons. Therefore, the lateral side and the lower back side of the head were usually exposed. The hair in those areas was maintained because it was still serving its purpose to keep the head warm. Consequently, early humans have never lost their hair in those areas. This is the reason that baldness never occurs on the lateral side and on the lower back side of the head.

Why does baldness occur as early as age thirty? This was because hunting in snowy and blizzard conditions was a very physical and harsh job. The job was predominantly carried out by young men who were stronger and more energetic. They started to wear hats for a considerable time of the year since beginning in their twenties and into their thirties, leading to early hair loss. Consequently, the genetic baldness trait often starts when men are in their thirties. No wonder we have difficulty determining why many perfectly healthy young men start losing their hair in their thirties.

My hat theory of baldness is also supported by the fact that European men still maintained big mustaches and bushy beards, even though they had become bald. This was because they could cover their heads with hats, but they could not cover their faces during their hunting trips, no matter how cold it might be. They needed to see and to breathe. This was why their mustaches and beards were maintained—to help keep their faces warm. In fact, their mustaches grew bigger and their beards became bushier, unlike the hair under their hats, which had been shed because it lost its usefulness.

Why do people in Norway have the highest frequency of baldness? It is because Norway was located in the center of ice field during the Ice Age. In other words, it was the coldest region in Europe. Thus, early settlers in that region had to wear hats all the time, leading to higher frequency of baldness among Norwegian men. It supports my theory that wearing hats was the cause of genetic baldness. The high frequency of baldness in Norway coincides with the high concentration of the blond hair and blue and green eyes people in that country. All these genetic traits were developed attributable to the extreme cold climate in the Baltic Sea region.

Why didn't European women develop baldness? It was because they didn't wear hats as the men did. Even though they all lived in the same cold climate, women spent most of their time inside their shelters. During those days, hunting was mainly carried out by men. Most women were not strong enough to hunt, and neither were there many fruits available for gathering in the tundra. Women's main responsibilities were likely preparing food for the men, making clothing from animal skins and furs, and taking care of the children. Most of their jobs were done inside their shelters, where it was warmer. Since they didn't spend much time outside, there was no need to wear hats all the time. Their hair remained to help keep their heads warm. As a result, baldness did not develop among early European women.

In Asia, the climate was seasonal. In wintertime, some men wore hats but not all the time, depending on how cold the region was. Consequently, some men developed baldness, just as European men did. Their baldness also occurred in the hairline above the forehead and on top of the head. This became a genetic trait among some Asian men. However, the frequency of baldness among Asian men is much lower than it is for European men because Asia was not as cold as Europe. People did not have to wear hats as much or for as long. Asian women seldom wore hats because of their hairstyles. Besides, many Asian people were superstitious and believed that wearing hats indoors could block prosperity from heaven. This is the reason few occurrences of baldness are found among Asian women, except for hair thinning due to old age.

In Africa, you would think that there should not be any baldness among African people, since it was so hot in the equatorial area that people did not have to wear hats to keep their heads warm. Contrarily, some people in Africa used hats to block the hot sun. Hats with large fringe offered shade and helped with cooling. Whether hats were worn depended on the area and the customs of the people. How long and how often they wore hats played a part in determining baldness; thus, people who wore hats for a considerable time of the year also developed hair loss because their hair had lost its purpose to block the hot sun. Consequently, baldness also became genetic among some African men but only among a few. This is why there are bald people among the African population.

SUMMARY: Although baldness is genetic and hereditary, not everyone in a family will inherit the gene. The gene of baldness was developed from wearing hats in different climates. However, it does not make people more adaptable to the climate. The truth is that baldness makes people more vulnerable to both hot and cold climates, not to mention the effect on self-image. Therefore, not all genes were developed for better reasons.

2.17

BODY HEIGHT

FACTS AND QUESTIONS: When we look at the body height of European, Asian, and African people, there is an average height difference among these three groups, except for some individuals with abnormal growth. European people are by far the tallest. They are much taller than Asian people. On average, they are about six inches (fifteen centimeters) taller than Asians. What caused early humans in Europe to grow taller that it became a genetic trait among them? African people are also taller than Asians, but they are not as tall as Europeans. Why are Asian people so much shorter than the rest?

If you observe carefully, then you will notice some interesting characteristics of body height in each group of people. European people are taller mainly because they have longer legs. Why do they have longer legs? Asians' torsos (the main body without the head and limbs) are not that much shorter than Europeans' torsos. They are shorter mainly because they have shorter legs. Most Asian people have long waists and short legs. What caused longer waists and shorter legs among Asians? This phenomenon is even more obvious among Japanese and Korean women. Why are they different from other Asians? African people usually have longer arms and legs but shorter torsos, which make them fast runners. Why do African people have long limbs?

Both environmental and genetic factors play important roles in the development of human height. In the recent two centuries, people have grown noticeably taller and bigger than their parents. This may be attributed to environmental factors, which include living standards, food and nutrition, medical access and overall health, livelihood and way of life, and so on. These factors are affecting human growth a great deal, resulting in a dramatic increase in human height. Although it varies in different regions and countries, height increases occur in all humans across the globe. However, genetic factors play a different role and set the basic framework for body height in each group of people. If we all came from the same ancestors, then why do we grow into different body heights in different continents?

MY THEORIES AND INTERPRETATIONS: We can reasonably predict that Europe was covered with snow for most of the year during the Ice Age. Early humans in Europe relied on hunting for food. Although reindeer were common throughout northern Europe, people had to chase herds of reindeer in the snow for long distances. If they had short legs, then they would not be able to move fast enough to follow the herd. Gradually, their bodies grew longer legs, so they could walk faster in the snow and avoid becoming stuck or sinking in the snow mass. Of course, this development was slow and gradual. Each generation grew slightly longer legs. Consequently, long legs became a genetic trait among European people. Therefore, Europeans' long legs were developed to increase their mobility in the snow. This was their adaptation to the snowy environment they lived in. This is similar to beavers in the wild that rely on fish for food and have developed bigger, stronger, and continuously growing front teeth to cut down trees to build dams in rivers to trap fish. They have also developed paddle-like tails to help them swim faster so that they can catch fish.

Similarly, in Africa, people developed short torsos with long arms and legs to help them survive in their habitat. Their livelihood depended on gathering and hunting in the savanna. Longer legs helped them walk longer distances and run faster. Shorter torsos helped them conserve energy, so they could spend more time under the sun. While gathering fruits from trees, longer arms and legs helped them reach higher. Their body framework became a genetic trait among African people. This is similar to a giraffe, which developed longer legs and a longer neck to reach foliage on higher branches.

In Asia, people's livelihoods relied on farming. The predominant agriculture in Asia was rice and vegetables. To grow rice at the early stage, you need fields totally covered with an inch of water. You plant each germinated rice plant separately into the wet mud. This planting takes days to do. You have to bend down on your knees in the field and move backward from one place to another. Planting vegetables was done the same way but on dry ground. At harvest time, people again have to bend down to do their work. For this kind of farming, people with smaller bodies and shorter legs are more suitable. It makes it easier for them to bend down and to stay down. A tall person with long legs would find it very difficult to do this kind of work. In addition, bending their bodies down constantly caused them to stretch their backs longer. Consequently, Asian people developed longer waists. Therefore, the small bodies, longer waists, and shorter legs of Asians were developed to adapt to their livelihood, making their farming life-style easier. These became genetic traits among Asian people.

Furthermore, traditional Chinese customs also played a role in the development of short legs. Before there were chairs, benches, and stools, people sat on the floor with their legs crossed over each other, or they knelt on the floor, which restricted leg growth. This tradition continued for thousands of years in China. This is why they developed shorter legs. In the early days, only high-ranking government officials sat in chairs. Peasants began to use benches and stools in the recent millennium. However, in Japan, people sat on the floor until the early twentieth century. As a result, they had shorter legs than the Chinese, who had abandoned this tradition a few hundred years earlier. When Europeans car-ried out trading in China in the nineteenth century, they called Japanese people dwarves. In the twentieth century, Japanese peo-ple recorded a rapid growth in body height, which correlated to the time of modernization and industrialization in Japan. People had abandoned the old tradition of sitting. They started using chairs and benches, which released the restriction of leg growth. Their dramatic increase in body height resulted from the growth of their legs.

Asian culture has also played a part in the development of long waists among Japanese and Korean people. Many Japanese and Korean females have noticeably longer waists. Their body frame-work was developed as a result of their traditional greeting. When they meet people, they always take a deep bow (bend their heads and upper bodies down) as a greeting or to show respect or sin-cerity. They do the same when they say farewell. This cultural practice created longer waists due to frequently bending the upper body down to near waist level. Longer waists are more noticeable among women than men. This was attributed to women being in the lower level of society. They had to bow to everyone, whereas men only bowed when it was necessary. Eventually, women in Japan and Korea developed longer waists, which became a genetic trait among them. (Note: This tradition originally began in China. Unfortunately, this elegant and graceful greeting was somehow lost in the Chinese culture, whereas the Japanese and Koreans, who had learned this culture from the Chinese, carried it well into the twentieth century.)

SUMMARY: The development of our facial traits tells the history of our ancestors and helps us understand their livelihoods, habitats, ways of life, diets, cultures, and so on. From body height, we learned that Europeans relied on hunting for food, Asians relied on farming, and African people depended on hunting and gathering in the savanna. This knowledge helps us understand the possible origin of some of the genetic makeups and diseases we have inherited. For example: the origin of genetic high cholesterol among some European people may be attributed to the hunting life of inland ancestors, who relied on game meat for food for tens of thousands of years. Red meat was their main diet, and they ate very little carbohydrates due to the cold climate that was unfavorable for growing vegetables and fruits. This may be why many Europeans have the genetic disease of high cholesterol. On the other hand, high cholesterol might not be a problem for some Europeans whose ancestors lived by the coast of the Atlantic Ocean and Mediterranean Sea because they ate more fish than meat and had more fruits and vegetables. Therefore, some genetic makeups may offer us some clues as to where your ancestors lived in the past. Asian people have fewer cholesterol problems due to their traditional diet. Their ancestors' main diet was rice, vegetables, fruits, and fish. Meat was a rare item for most of them. That's why they had lower levels of cholesterol, which became a genetic trait among Asians.

We also begin to understand the genetic disease of some arthritis. Arthritis seems to be more common among European people than Asian people. This may be attributed to the body height of early humans. There is cartilage at the end of each bone in the joint area. When the cartilage is worn, bone rubs on bone, causing pain and arthritis. Why do European people have early worn-down knee and hip cartilages? This may be attributed to their longer legs, which were developed to walk in the snow during their earlier hunting life. Long legs put more torque on a joint, just like a long-arm wrench, causing more force and damage to the cartilage. Explanation: when a short-arm wrench cannot turn a rusty old nut, we use a long-arm wrench to turn it because a long-arm wrench gives more torque and power to turn the nut. Europeans' bigger and heavier bodies also add more weight and pressure to the joint, causing early wear down of the cartilage. This led to the development of a genetic weakness of cartilage among European people. Because Asian ancestors had shorter legs that caused less torque to and force on the joints, this resulted in less damage to the cartilage. Together with their smaller bodies and lighter body weight, their cartilage lasts longer. Consequently, Asian people have genetically healthier joints.

2.18

SUMMARY AND CONCLUSIONS

Many factors have caused changes to human faces since their early days. Among them, the most important process was adaptation. Because early humans migrated from continent to continent, they faced changing climates and environments. To survive, they had to make changes to their bodies, so they became better suited to their new habitats. Some of the most important adaptations of early humans include the following:

1. European people developed down-facing, narrow nostrils to help keep warm body air in and cold air out to adapt to the cold climate in Europe.
2. African people developed large, round nostrils to help cool their bodies and to adapt to the hot climate in Africa.
3. Europeans developed large eyes with blue and green irises to enhance their vision in the dark environment inside their shelters.
4. To compensate for this extreme change to their irises, Europeans had to move their eyeballs slightly inward into the eye sockets to provide some shade for their light-colored eyes. They also developed big eyelids and grew thicker eyebrows and longer eyelashes to reduce sun glare and snow

reflection so that their vision would not be blurred by bright light in outdoor environments.

5. African people developed dark skin to protect their bodies from UV radiation damage.

6. Africans shed their body hair to help cool their bodies and to adapt to the hot sun in Africa.

7. Europeans increased their hair to keep their heads warm and grew big mustaches and bushy beards to keep their faces warm in order to adapt to the bitterly cold climate in Europe.

8. African people developed tubular hair shafts to provide more shade for their heads. Tubular hair shafts produce spiral and coiled hair, which helped their heads stay cooler in the hot sun.

9. Europeans developed longer legs to help their mobility on the snowy ground, whereas African people developed longer limbs to help with hunting and gathering in the savanna.

10. Asian people developed smaller bodies with short legs and long waists to adapt to farming life.

Besides adaptation, humans' daily habits and behaviors (if they persisted for many generations in a group of people) also caused changes in their facial traits and body characteristics. For example:

1. European people developed high and narrow noses with pointed nose tips due to blowing their noses frequently in a cold climate.

2. African people developed low and wide noses with fleshy, round nose tips due to pressing down on the nose bridge frequently while wiping the sweat from their faces because of a hot climate.

3. Europeans also developed thin lips due to clenching their mouths tight and pulling their lips inward all the time because of the extremely cold weather in Europe.

4. Africans developed bigger and fuller lips due to leaving their mouths open and their lips hanging freely to help with breathing and the cooling of their bodies in a very hot continent.

5. European people developed narrow and long face shapes because of sleeping sideways in cold weather, whereas Asian and African people developed rounder and wider face shapes because of sleeping facing up in a hot climate.

6. Asian people's farming lifestyle caused longer waists and shorter legs because of bending and kneeling down during cultivations.

Among environmental factors, climate is the most important factor to affect humans directly and indirectly. Beside what I have described previously, other changes include the following:

1. European people developed light skin due to low levels of sun exposure as a result of prolonged living in dark caves and wearing thick clothing because of the extremely cold weather in Europe.

2. European people developed blond and red hair attributable to a lower production of black eumelanin due to a lack of sunlight exposure that resulted from continuous living in dark shelters because of a cold climate.

3. African and Asian people developed black hair due to high concentrations of black eumelanin, which was produced to protect them from UV radiation and intense sunlight.

4. European people have oval hair shafts and wavy hair, which developed as a result of growing longer hair to keep the neck and shoulders warm in a cold climate.

5. Baldness among European men is attributed to wearing hats in a cold climate.
6. The straight and aligned front teeth of European people are attributable to closing their lips tight because of a cold climate.

Regional cultures and traditions also caused changes in facial traits and body characteristics among a large group of people. For example:

1. More than one billion people in northern Asia have developed slender eyes, small eyelids with little mobility, thin and loose eyebrows, and short eyelashes, all of which are attributable to the traditional Chinese hairstyle. Their less pronounced cheekbones and fewer wrinkles on the forehead are also attributed to this hairstyle.
2. The traditional Chinese custom of sitting on the floor restricted leg growth, resulting in shorter legs among people in Korea, Japan, and Mongolia.
3. The traditional Asian greeting caused longer waists among Japanese and Korean females.
4. Asian people's straight hair with round hair shafts also resulted from the traditional Chinese hairstyle.

In addition, regional diet was a genetic factor that caused bad and good teeth among different groups of people. For example:

1. Asian people have genetically bad teeth due to prolific production of sweet fruits in Asia. The ways in which they bit and cut fruits with their front teeth led to the development of buck teeth among many Asian people.
2. Europeans inherited good teeth due to drinking milk and a lack of sweet fruits in a cold climate.

Language can also affect our facial characteristics. The two slightly protruded upper front teeth among Japanese people are attributed to their language, because many Japanese pronunciations require their tongues to touch the back of their upper front teeth. In addition, motherhood led to the development of concave cheeks and high and prominent cheekbones among women, making their cheeks more suitable for resting a baby's head.

As you can see, not all changes are attributed to climate and adaptation. People's livelihoods, diets, daily habits, behaviors, ways of life, cultures, hairstyles, and even languages and motherhood all have played important roles in the modification of human faces. Some changes began soon after people settled in a new continent. Others occurred much later when people started to develop their cultures and civilizations. All of these exhibit interesting and fascinating stories of our ancestors.

When you combine all these changes, each group of people has created distinct facial and body characteristics that distinguish them from other groups of people. When you look at modern-day Europeans, with their big blue and green eyes, high and narrow noses, and white skin with blond hair, they look so obviously different from other groups of people. You can't help but think they might have come from different ancestral stock. The fact is that all their traits were developed because of the extremely cold climate in Europe, not because of biological separation. In other words, they did not descend from a different lineage.

My theories and interpretations of the development of facial traits among each group of people are logical and straightforward.

They are based on our daily life and how we behave in a similar environment. They simply make sense. Most important of all, there are no contradictions in my interpretations. The facial traits of European people were developed consistently due to the cold climate in Europe, whereas the facial traits of African people were developed consistently due to the hot climate in Africa. Asian people's traits, which represent intermediate changes between the Europeans and the Africans, were developed as a result of a mild and seasonal climate in Asia.

Every facial trait is a gene. Of course, there are differences in genetic makeup among different groups of people. However, it's a very small amount of our genome. Human beings have about twenty thousand to twenty-five thousand genes (Internet source). For all the differences in facial traits and outer appearances, it is not enough to classify any group of people as a new species or subspecies, nor can it separate people in the world biologically, other than men and women. **European, Asian, and African people look different from one another mainly because they evolved differently to adapt to the climates and environments in which they lived, not because they descended from different human stocks. We all came from the same ancestors.**

CHAPTER 3

DEVELOPMENT OF FACIAL TRAITS AMONG
MIDDLE EASTERN AND INDIAN PEOPLE

Middle Eastern and Indian people are two other large groups of people in the world. Their populations have now reached 1.5 billion people. They have developed their own facial characteristics that distinguish them from European, Asian, and African people. In this chapter, you will learn how and why they have developed their facial traits.

GEOGRAPHIC DISTRIBUTION OF MIDDLE EASTERN AND INDIAN PEOPLE: Middle Eastern people's ancestors were indigenous to the Middle Eastern area. Most of the Middle East is situated south of 40° latitude north and lies on both sides of the Tropic of Cancer. This area includes all countries extending from the eastern Mediterranean Sea and across the Arabian Peninsula to Afghanistan in the east, and it also includes countries in northern Africa on the southern shore of the Mediterranean. Middle Eastern people described in this chapter do not include black people of African origin whose facial traits are described in chapter 2. Indian people are those whose ancestors were indigenous to the Indian Peninsula, including India, Pakistan, Bangladesh,

118

Sri Lanka, and Nepal. (Note: Indian people described in this chapter do not include Native American Indians.)

CLIMATE OF THE MIDDLE EAST AND INDIA: Even though the Middle East lies on both sides of the Tropic of Cancer, quite a distance north of the equator, its climate is generally very hot and dry. Most areas are desert or semidesert environment. Except for the Nile Delta in Egypt and the area northwest of the Persian Gulf, most areas do not have rivers to support irrigation for large agriculture. It has little forest or vegetation. Areas in northern Africa are mostly desert, except for a narrow zone south of the Mediterranean Sea where a warm climate prevails.

India has a wide range of climates. Even though it has four seasons, winter is short and mild and only occurs in northern India. This is because the highest mountain range in the world, the Himalaya Mountains, separates the cold climate of Tibet from the tropical climate of India. Except for the arid desert in the northwestern area of India, most regions are wet with monsoon rain from June to September. Even though the Indian Peninsula is situated north of the equator, its weather is more closely related to an equatorial climate than a tropical climate. Generally speaking, the Indian Peninsula is hot and humid.

SCOPE OF DESCRIPTION: With a population of one billion people in India and a half billion in the Middle East, undoubtedly, there are wide variations in facial characteristics. The facial traits described in this chapter are common characteristics of Middle Eastern and Indian people. It does not mean that all people must have the same features. Similar facial characteristics may also occur among other groups of people but may have developed for different reasons. Besides, many people do not know that they have ancestors from other regions. They may bear facial features slightly different from their own groups of people. Furthermore, descendants of mixed marriages will have mixed facial characteristics. As you read this chapter, please remember that my descriptions and interpretations apply only to people who are truly descendants of Middle Eastern or Indian ancestry.

WHO WERE THE ANCESTORS OF MIDDLE EASTERN AND INDIAN PEOPLE? According to archaeological findings, early humans migrated to the Arabian Peninsula from Africa as early as 125,000 years ago. About seventy thousand years ago, another large group of early humans began their great migration from Africa to Asia. They crossed over to the Arabian Peninsula, passed through the deserts in the Middle East, and followed the Ganges River south of the Himalaya Mountains to the door of Southeast Asia. Neither time did they settle in the Middle East or India. I have come to this conclusion based on analyses of facial traits and have developed the following hypotheses:

1. The facial traits of Middle Eastern and Indian people have very little similarity to African people. For example, Middle Eastern and Indian people have high and narrow noses with oval nostrils and big movable eyelids, whereas African people have low and wide noses with round nostrils and the absence of big movable eyelids. We must remember that the climate in the Middle East and India was very similar to Africa. Both had tropical and equatorial climates. In other words, if early humans from Africa remained and settled in the Middle East and India, then they would maintain their low and wide noses with big round nostrils. They would not have developed high and narrow noses and big movable

eyelids. There are more facial traits supporting this hypothesis, which will be described later in this chapter.

2. Early humans might have possessed the spiritual belief that the rising sun would lead them to a better life. (This is described more fully in chapter 4.) That was the reason they continued their journey eastward in the direction of the rising sun without settling in the Middle East and India. Their migration ended when they arrived in Asia, a place with mild weather, plenty of fruit trees, and water.

If early humans from Africa did not stay in the Middle East and India during their earlier migrations, then who could be the ancestors of Middle Eastern and Indian people? When did they arrive in this region?

I believe that the ancestors of Middle Eastern and Indian people came from Northern Europe. (Note: other scientists may have come to same conclusion using different information.) About twenty-two thousand years ago, the last glaciation of the recent Ice Age had reached its peak (Dunbar and Waage, *Historical Geology*). The glacier covered the entire northern and central Europe. Most regions of Europe became unbearably cold. Early Europeans could no longer stay in such a cold environment. Gradually, people started to leave and moved south to warmer areas. Hence, this triggered a great migration of European people.

They found warmer climates in the region now called the Middle East. Many of them stayed and settled along the eastern shore of the Mediterranean Sea. Some migrated farther south and returned to Africa. They found their settlement area on the northern coast of the African continent, along the southern coast of the Mediterranean Sea.

The desert and semidesert environment of the Middle East had very little vegetation or rivers. Life was difficult for European migrants, who were still hunters and gatherers then. Except for the narrow area along the Mediterranean coast where they might find fish for food, most places were barren land of desert sand. Many European migrants decided to continue their journey eastward, even though it was long and difficult to cross a wide area of deserts and semideserts. Before they reached India, some of them might have already become exhausted and decided to settle in areas now known as Iraq, Iran, and Afghanistan. This group of European migrants, together with those who settled along the coastal area of the Mediterranean Sea, became the ancestors of Middle Eastern people.

The remaining large group of European migrants continued their eastward migration. Their journey ended when they reached the Himalaya Mountains, a mountain range so high they couldn't cross it. At the time of disappointment, they found the big Ganges River south of the Himalayas. The Ganges is the largest river in India with abundant fish. It provided them with water and food. The weather was hot and humid but great. It was exactly what the migrants were looking for. The Ganges became their final migration destination. They settled, and their population multiplied. Over time, some of them moved farther south to occupy the entire Indian Peninsula. They became the ancestors of the Indian people. (Note: The Ganges is the most sacred river in India and is known to have given Indian people guidance and a lifeline for thousands of years. I believe that its history might date back as far as twenty-two thousand years ago.) European migrants might not have settled in India if the Ganges had not offered them new life and hope and neither would they have thrived, becoming a nation of one billion people.

DEVELOPMENT OF FACIAL TRAITS AMONG MIDDLE EASTERN AND INDIAN PEOPLE: Before early Europeans started their migration to the Middle East and India, their ancestors had been settled in northern Europe for more than twenty thousand years. They had already developed European traits and no longer looked like their African ancestors. They had high and narrow noses with narrow nostrils, big blue and green eyes, big movable eyelids with long eyelashes, light skin and blond hair, thin lips, and narrow and long face shapes. Women had high and pronounced cheekbones, whereas men had big mustaches and bushy beards, and many men had some type of baldness. These facial characteristics had already become genetic traits among them before their migration.

When they arrived in the Middle East and India, they found the place where they wanted to settle. It was much warmer than northern Europe. However, they quickly found that they faced some difficulties in their new environment. The climate was extremely different from where they came from. The Middle East was very hot and dry, whereas India was very hot and humid. Their bodies couldn't take the extreme heat; their skin burned, and their eyes couldn't see under the bright desert sun. To survive, they had to make themselves more suitable for their new environment. Human beings have a high capability to adapt. To adjust to the new environment, their bodies had to make some changes. Of course, these physical changes were gradual and slow. Over time, their new facial and body characteristics became more pronounced. They no longer looked like Europeans. They formed a new set of distinct facial traits, which distinguish the Middle Eastern and Indian people from all other groups of people, including their European ancestors. In the following sections, I'll describe my theories and interpretations of how Middle Eastern and Indian people developed new facial traits from their European ancestry. (Note: to understand this chapter better, it is best to read chapter 2 first.)

3.1—OVAL NOSTRILS: European migrants had narrow nostrils, which were developed in the cold climate in Europe. Narrow nostrils helped European people to maintain their body temperature by keeping the warm body air in and by slowing down the cold air from rushing into their lungs. (See section 2.2—NOSTRILS for more details.) In the Middle East and India, the climate was very hot. They needed to disperse their body heat to help with cooling. Narrow nostrils had the disadvantage of not letting the hot body air to exhale quickly. Normally, human beings disperse their body heat through perspiration. However, nostrils provide twenty-four-hour continuous ventilation to regulate our body temperature. To survive in a very hot climate, early migrants needed to develop bigger nostrils. This is why Middle Eastern and Indian people have developed oval nostrils to allow more ventilation to cool their bodies. Southern India featured an equatorial climate that was very hot and humid. People in those areas have developed almost round nostrils. The oval and oval/round nostrils became genetic traits among Middle Eastern and Indian people, which distinguish them from European people.

3.2—HIGH NOSES, SLIGHTLY WIDER AND FLESHIER: European migrants had high and narrow noses with pointed nose tips, which were developed as a result of blowing their noses frequently because of colds. (See section 2.1—NOSES for more details.) When they settled in the Middle East and India, they had fewer colds because of the hot climate, and they didn't have to blow their noses as frequently. Without pressing their noses from both sides with their fingers as often, their noses became slightly wider and not as narrow as their European ancestors. Wider noses provided larger nasal passages, which helped with cooling the body by allowing hot body air to exit quickly. Together with the oval nostrils, these new features helped the migrants to adapt to the hot climate in the Middle East and India. Without pressing the nose as frequently, fatty tissues accumulated in the nose area, developing fleshier noses. Over time, the high and narrow noses with pointed nose tips of the early European migrants gradually changed to slightly wider and fleshier noses because of the hot climate. This is why Middle Eastern and Indian people have high noses, but they are slightly wider and fleshier than the noses of European people.

In southern India, it was hot and humid due to the monsoon rains. People sweat all the time. When they wiped the sweat from their faces, they unconsciously pressed the nose bridge downward. Over time, they developed broader and slightly lower nose bridges with bigger and more rounded nostrils. This is a facial characteristic commonly seen among some southern Indian people. You don't find this type of nose among Middle Eastern people. People in the Middle East didn't sweat as much due to the dry weather, even though it was hot there. Since they didn't have to wipe the sweat from their faces, they didn't press down their nose bridges. This is why Middle Eastern people still maintain the high noses of their European ancestors.

3.3—HOOKED NOSES: A hooked nose is also known as a Roman nose, an arched nose, an aquiline nose, or an eagle nose. Although hooked noses are found in every group of people and everywhere in the world, they are usually rare. The characteristic of hooked noses has been considered to correlate to higher intelligence, stronger personality, nobility, and the trait of philosopher or noble warrior by some ethnic groups. There are no actual biological links to all these hypotheses. Hooked noses are a distinct feature among many people in the Middle East that distinguishes them from other groups of people. Why do many people in the Middle East have hooked noses? Until now, there are no scientific explanations as to the origin and development of hooked noses.

My theory is that the hooked noses of Middle Eastern people were developed to prevent their face scarves or veils from falling down. In a desert environment, it was necessary for people to protect their faces from sandstorms and from the intense sun, especially for European migrants who had light skin when they arrived in the desert. Consequently, Middle Eastern people often used face scarves and veils to cover their faces. The nose is formed of cartilage and soft tissues, and its shape can be altered under prolonged and continuous external pressure. When you tie the scarf or veil tight behind the head, it presses the upper part of the nose bridge downward to form a slight low. Thus, the middle portion of the nose bridge developed higher to prevent the veil from sliding downward. Together with the pointed nose tip (a characteristic of a European nose), they formed hooked noses. This modification of their noses was developed to help keep the scarf from falling down. Just like we develop calluses in our hands to protect against abrasion when we do construction work with bare hands. Many species in the wild have developed special features to adapt to their environments. For example, horses developed longer legs to run faster in the savanna, mountain sheep and goats developed unique hoof structures to adapt to the steep mountain terrain, and fish developed scales to protect their soft bodies and help them swim faster with flexibility. Since face scarves and veils were very useful in the desert environment, people wore them all the time. Consequently, most people developed hooked noses, which became a genetic trait among Middle Eastern people after many generations. Hooked noses are also found among Indian people but are much less common. Because desert environment is found only in the northwestern region of India.

Assuming that my theory is correct, the development of hooked noses might not have occurred among the early settlers before the end of the Ice Age because the material available for making face scarves and veils was not available then. Hooked noses were likely developed after people started practicing agriculture. By then, they had wool to make fabric and cotton to make cloth. Trade merchants had brought silk from the orient via the Silk Road. The tradition of wearing facial scarves and veils gradually became a part of their culture. Later, it also became a requirement of some religions.

Before people of the Middle East and India used face scarves and veils, how did they protect their faces from intense sunlight and sand dust? Early European migrants had to make many changes and modifications to adapt to the hot desert environment, which led to the development of new facial traits among them. They are described as follows:

3.4—DARK SKIN PIGMENTATION: When European people left Europe, heading south to a warmer place, they had already developed light skin, which was developed due to low sunlight exposure in their dark shelters and wearing thick clothing in the cold climate. (See section 2.12—SKIN COLOR for more details.) As they approached the Middle East and India, the weather became so hot that they could no longer wear their furs and animal skins. When they stripped their clothing to help with cooling, their bodies were exposed to the intense sunlight. Their light skin burned and was damaged by UV radiation. To adapt to the high sunlight exposure, they needed to produce more melanin, predominantly eumelanin, to protect their skin from UV radiation damage. To change the genetic makeup of low melanin production (most Europeans had low eumelanin production attributed to prolonged living in dark shelters in a cold climate) was not an easy process. It is different from suntanning, which changes a person's skin color in just a few days but is not a genetic change of skin pigmentation.

After living in an environment with high levels of sunlight exposure in the Middle East for many generations, descendants of early European migrants gradually began to produce more eumelanin genetically. As eumelanin increased, their skin took on a darker pigmentation. Dark skin with high eumelanin can disperse UV radiation and reduce the damage. This is why Middle Eastern and Indian people have developed dark skin pigmentation, which was a necessity for people living in regions with strong sunlight. Of course, there are variations in skin pigmentation among Middle Eastern people. Those who lived in a cooler climate in the northern area of the Middle East commonly had light and medium skin pigmentations due to lower sunlight exposure attributed to wearing more clothing for longer periods of time. Skin pigmentation increased and became darker as people migrated south, closer to tropical and equatorial areas. This is clearly shown among southern Indian people whose skin pigmentation is almost as dark as African people.

3.5—BLACK HAIR: European migrants had light hair color, such as blond, red, and brown. After they had settled in the Middle

East and India for many generations, their bodies started to produce more melanin to protect their skin from the strong sun. Melanin consists of black and brown eumelanin. Black eumelanin is most effective to protect human skin from UV radiation damage. It is reasonable to predict that most Middle Eastern and Indian people had high concentrations of black eumelanin as shown in their dark skin pigmentation. As a result, their hair also shared higher amounts of black eumelanin, leading to black hair. This is why most Middle Eastern and Indian people have black hair. The changes in hair color from light to black were not limited to the hair of the head; it also evolved with the color of the eyebrow, eyelash, mustache, beard, and body hair.

3.6—DARK-BROWN EYES: When European migrants arrived in the Middle East, their blue and green eyes couldn't tolerate the bright sunlight. They couldn't keep their eyes open without squinting. In the desert, there was little vegetation and grass to absorb or reduce the bright sunlight. The reflection from the sand made the sunlight more bright and intense, which blurred their vision. Their bodies gradually replaced their blue and green irises with dark-brown irises to reduce the amount of light entering the pupils. This is similar to how we replace light-colored curtains with dark-colored curtains to reduce the amount of light entering a room. (See section 2.4—EYE COLOR for more details.) The change of iris color was gradual and might have taken a long time. It might have occurred in different stages. Since the color of the iris was formed of different shades and rays of color, blue and green would be subdued as they were gradually replaced by brown. Finally, their irises became dark brown. Dark-brown irises reduced sun glare just like our sunglasses do today. Therefore, the dark-brown eyes of Middle Eastern and Indian people were developed to adapt to the bright sunlight in the desert and tropical environment. However, in areas of less intense sunlight, people might have maintained light-colored irises. This is why some Middle Eastern people still have bluish and greenish eyes.

3.7—LONGER, BUSHIER, BLACK EYEBROWS: You may wonder why Middle Eastern and Indian people have very long, bushy, black eyebrows. Of course, eyebrows prevent sweat from running down into the eyes as well as dust from falling into the eyes from above. Long and bushy eyebrows served the Indian people well, as they sweat a lot due to their hot and humid weather. For Middle Eastern people who lived in a desert environment, they also helped to prevent sand dust from entering the eyes. Most important of all, long dark eyebrows reduce the glare from the sun. Sun glare is so intense in the desert that even those with dark-brown eyes had difficulty tolerating the brightness. It blurred their vision and caused damage to the eyes. In those days, people did not have sunglasses to reduce sun glare. To adapt to the bright sunlight, people grew longer and more bushy eyebrows to help absorb the sunlight and reduce the glare. The original light-colored eyebrows of early migrants gradually changed to black as their bodies produced more eumelanin. Black eyebrows absorbed light and greatly helped reduce the glare. This is why Middle Eastern and Indian people have grown very long, bushy black eyebrows, which eventually became a genetic trait among them.

3.8—LONGER AND THICKER EYELASHES: In the desert, people had to protect their eyes from the blowing sand and to reduce the sunlight from above and the reflection from the sand. Early settlers in the Middle East and India needed all the help they could get to reduce blurred vision and to protect their eyes. Eyelashes can prevent sand dust from entering the eye, provide shade for the eyes from sunlight, and reduce the reflection from the sand. For people living in a desert environment, the longer and thicker the eyelashes, the better. This is why Middle Eastern and Indian people had very long and thick eyelashes. They were grown to adapt to the bright sunlight and the desert environment in the Middle East. This theory is fully supported by the fact that the camel has grown long and thick eyelashes for the same reasons. Every feature of the camel is specially designed to help it survive in the desert environment.

3.9—BUSHY BLACK BEARDS AND MUSTACHES: European men had genetically light-colored bushy beards and big mustaches, which were grown to keep their faces and chins warm in the cold European climate. This feature has become a trait of European men. When they settled in the hot Middle East and India, you would think that their bodies would shed the beard and mustache to help with cooling. Why did they maintain the bushy beard and mustache?

There are several reasons that may explain why Middle Eastern and Indian people maintained bushy beards and mustaches. First, before early settlers began to use scarves and veils to protect their faces, thick beards could protect their light-skinned faces from sunburn. Since northern Europeans couldn't change their light-skinned pigmentation quickly to protect their faces from sunburn, thick beards offered shade for the lower half of their faces and helped to prevent sunburn.

Second, thick beards and big mustaches helped protect their faces from blowing sand. Sandstorms occurred often in the desert. Blowing sand could blind the eyes and abrade the face if they were not covered. Thick beards helped protect the face from a direct hit by blowing sand. This is why most Middle Eastern men kept their beards and mustaches in the desert environment. This tradition might have begun as early as European migrants settled in the Middle East. After the end of the Ice Age, people began using facial scarves and veils to protect their faces. However, the custom of having beards and mustaches continued until modern day because it has become a part of Middle Eastern culture.

Third, the white-skinned faces of early migrants also reflected sunlight into their light-colored eyes. Keeping long and bushy beards helped absorb the sunlight and reduce the reflection from their faces. It became more effective when their light-colored beards changed to a black color, which absorbed more sunlight.

Fourth, the climate in India was quite different from the desert environment in the Middle East. There are no widespread deserts in India, except for the northwestern area. Most regions in India are hot and humid with thick vegetation. Early settlers didn't have to protect their faces from blowing sand, but they still needed beards to protect their faces from sunburn. Although most modern Indian men are clean shaven without a beard, we can be certain that they have beards by looking at the beard roots on their faces. Over time, descendants of early settlers gradually took on dark skin pigmentation. They had less need for thick beards to protect their faces. In areas of high humidity, thick beards and mustaches were not practical. It was too hot and unbearable. Men started to shave their beards and mustaches to help with cooling. This traditional custom of a clean-shaven face eventually became a part of Indian culture. (Note: Indian and Pakistani people have very similar facial traits and likely share similar ancestry. They are separated mainly because of their different cultures and religious beliefs. In appearance, it is hard to distinguish which country they belong to. However, you can generally guess their nationality by whether they have beard or not. Most Pakistani men have beard, which is a part of Pakistani culture, whereas most Indian men are usually clean shaven as part of Indian culture.)

The trait of bushy beards and mustaches among Middle Eastern and Indian men also indicates European ancestry. If they migrated from Africa directly, then they would not have developed bushy beards because they already had dark skin and dark-brown eyes to protect against the intense sunlight.

3.10—HAIRLINE ENCROACHMENT IN THE FOREHEAD AREA, A UNIQUE TRAIT OF INDIAN WOMEN: Men had grown thick beards and big mustaches to protect their faces from sunburn and reduce the glare of bright sunlight. What could have helped European women protect their faces from sunburn and reduce sun glare in India? If you observe carefully, then you will notice that Indian women have very low hairlines, and the hairline on both sides of their foreheads has grown closer together, covering most of their temples. The reason for this encroachment is to reduce the amount of bare skin on the forehead, which otherwise would be exposed to full sun. Increasing the area of hair coverage protected their light forehead skin from sunburn. Hair also absorbed sunlight and reduced the glare for their light-colored eyes. Hairline encroachment is a trait commonly seen among Indian women, which distinguishes them from females of other groups of people. It became a genetic trait among them. Today, Indian women still bear this distinct trait, even though they now have dark skin and dark-brown eyes. It is not known whether Middle Eastern women have the same feature, since their culture has prohibited them to show their faces in public.

The development of a lower and closer hairline likely occurred at an early time, while the settlers still had fair skin that needed protection from the sun and UV radiation damage. This prediction regarding the time frame is logical, because if they had already developed dark skin pigmentation, then they would not need to grow hair in the forehead area for protection against the sun. Therefore, the process of changing from white skin to dark skin likely took a long time before it became genetic. The trait of hairline encroachment among Indian women firmly supports my theory of European ancestry. They would not have developed this trait if they came directly from Africa because they would have had dark skin to protect their foreheads.

3.11—DARK CIRCLES AROUND THE EYES, A UNIQUE TRAIT OF MIDDLE EASTERN PEOPLE: Another distinct facial characteristic of Middle Eastern people is the dark circles around their eyes. Why did they develop dark skin pigmentation around their eyes? In the desert, the sun is bright and intense without any shade. Early settlers in the Middle East had tried so hard to help their light-colored eyes by developing dark-brown irises, longer and bushier eyebrows, and longer and thicker eyelashes to help reduce the glare of bright sunlight. Unfortunately, these modifications were not enough to reduce the glare, especially for those who had light-skinned faces, which reflected more light into their eyes. What else could they do to further reduce the glare? They didn't have enough black eumelanin to change their faces to darker pigmentation during their early settlement time. So they concentrated the small amount of eumelanin they had around the eyes, which helped them to absorb light and reduce reflection from their light-skinned faces. Consequently, Middle Eastern people gradually developed darker skin pigmentation around their eyes, which helped them to adapt to the bright sunlight environment. Later, it became a genetic trait among Middle Eastern people. This trait is more noticeable among women than men because men have bushy beards to help reduce the sun glare, whereas women's faces are bare, with little facial hair except for eyebrows. Thus, they have a greater need for darker skin around their eyes to help reduce the glare. This modification probably developed during an early time, while they still had light skin and light-colored eyes. This feature is also found among Indian people, but it is not easily visible because of their very dark skin. (Note: Today, women like to put makeup around their eyes to make them more attractive, not realizing that their eye makeup also helps to reduce sun glare. Most women do not understand why they don't need to wear sunglasses as often when they wear eye makeup.)

The trait of dark eye circles strongly supports my theory that Middle Eastern and Indian people were migrants from Europe. They developed dark eye circles because of their light eyes and light skin. If they came directly from Africa, then there would be no need to develop dark eye circles because they already had dark eyes and dark-skinned faces.

3.12—LESS BALDNESS AMONG MEN: Many male migrants from Europe had genetic baldness. (See section 2.16—BALDNESS for more details.) The hereditary baldness among European men was attributable to wearing hats in the cold climate. Since their hats helped to keep their heads warm, their hair lost its purpose of keeping the head warm, leading to hair loss at an early age. When early European migrants arrived in the Middle East and India, they abandoned their fur hats because it was too hot to wear them. Their bald heads became vulnerable to sunburn. In desert and semidesert environments, there were few trees to provide shade for early migrants. It is not known what they used to provide shade for their heads in the desert in the early days. Nevertheless, they needed to protect their bald heads. To adapt to the hot sun environment, they grew more hair to cover their baldness. Over time, they had reversed the genetic baldness to full-grown hair. This is why there is less baldness among Middle Eastern and Indian men than among European men. (Note: a locally higher percentage of baldness in some regions of the Middle East may be related to present-day stress, diet, and extreme weather and health, not necessary due to genetics.)

After the Ice Age, cotton fabric and silk became available to humans. Middle Eastern and Indian people began to use them to cover their heads and necks for protection against the hot sun and to prevent sand and dust from settling in their hair. Head dressings were very useful in their environment, and they became traditional and customary. This led to a great diversity of headwear in the Middle East and India, such as keffiyeh for men and hijab for women, as well as kerchiefs and turbans, which became a part of their culture and religious dressing.

3.13—FULL AND FLESHY LIPS: Before European people migrated to the Middle East and India, they had genetically thin lips attributable to the cold climate in Europe. Because they had to close their mouths tight to help keep the warm body air in and to prevent cold air rushing into their mouths, this led to the development of thin lips. (See section 2.8—LIPS for more details.) When they settled in the Middle East and India, there was no need to keep their mouths closed because of the hot climate. In fact, they needed to keep their mouths open to help cool their bodies by allowing hot body air to exit freely. When they left their mouths open, their lips were free to grow fuller. Fatty tissues gradually increased in their lips, leading to full and fleshy lips. This modification of lips among Middle Eastern and Indian settlers reversed their ancestral thin lips to full and fleshy lips. In southern India where the climate was more hot and humid, people had kept their mouths open constantly, which led to even fuller and fleshier lips. This feature makes Indians the only group of people to have high noses with full and fleshy lips. It distinguishes them from the European people who have high noses but thin lips as well as the African people who have full lips but low noses.

3.14—SLIGHTLY WIDER FACES: Most European people have narrow and long face shapes, which were developed by sleeping sideways. (See section 2.11—FACE SHAPE for more details.) Sleeping sideways helped them stay warmer during the night by folding the body closer together. In a hot climate, this sleeping position trapped body heat and prevented it from dispersing, which made them uncomfortable during the night. People started to sleep facing up with both arms spread on the sides of body, thus allowing body heat to disperse while they slept. When sleeping facing up with the back of the head rested on the pillow, the sides of the head were not pressed and had a chance to develop wider. This is why Middle Eastern and Indian people have slightly wider faces than European people.

3.15—SMALLER BODY SIZE AMONG INDIANS: After the Ice Age, people in India started to practice agriculture, since the hot climate with plenty of rainfall made it favorable for farming. Farmwork required people to kneel down and to bend their bodies. Like Asian people, they have developed a smaller body size to adapt to this new way of life. After thousands of years of farming life, Indian people have smaller body sizes as compared to their European ancestors.

3.16—MAINTAIN GENETIC HIGH NOSES, BIG EYES, AND BIG EYELIDS: There are several genetic traits of European migrants that were maintained without any significant modifications, such as high noses, big eyes, big movable eyelids, bushy beards, and mustaches. Because these features helped them to adapt to the environment in the Middle East and India, it was not necessary to change them. For example, big movable eyelids helped them to prevent sand dust and controlled the amount of sunlight entering the eyes. High noses gave lateral shade for their eyes to reduce the glare. High nose bridges also served to prevent their facial scarves from falling down. Although there was no specific purpose for maintaining big eyes, there was no need to modify them either. So, they were maintained. Bushy beards and mustaches were maintained to protect their faces from blowing sand and intense sunlight. All these traits remained as hereditary. They also suggest European ancestry. If they migrated from Africa directly, then they would not have developed these facial characteristics.

3.17—MAINTAIN THE HAIRY BODY OF EUROPEAN ANCESTORS: European migrants had dense body hair, which might have helped early settlers to reduce sunburn. It is similar to our scalp, which seldom gets sunburned because it is protected by our hair, while our face often gets sunburned. This is why the genetic hairy bodies of European migrants were maintained.

SUMMARY AND CONCLUSION: The development of facial traits among Middle Eastern and Indian people clearly demonstrates that hereditary traits are not permanent. For example, the white skin and blond hair of European people, the most distinct features of European traits, have been changed to dark skin and black hair among settlers in India. This strongly supports that our facial traits can be altered, modified, and changed over time when a group of people settle in a new environment for a long time. Human beings will make changes to survive and to adapt. When the changes and modifications became more pronounced, they would look different from their ancestors. They became a new group of people with different facial traits.

In this chapter, you learned how Middle Eastern and Indian people developed their unique traits from their European ancestors. In chapter 2, you learned how the early humans in Europe developed European traits from their African ancestors. Asian people also developed Asian traits that distinguished them from their African ancestors. Some Asian people later migrated to Australia, North America, South America, and the islands in the Pacific Ocean. All of them have developed their own physical characteristics in their new settlement areas.

Our world consists of many climatic zones with extremely different environments and habitats. **Early humans had to make changes to their bodies to survive and thrive in various environments, leading to the development of different groups of people with different facial and body characteristics. This is why people look different in different regions of the world.**

C H A P T E R   4

THE JOURNEY OF EARLY HUMANS

    About 195,000 years ago, a group of early humans emerged along the Omo River in the Kibish Mountain area, southwestern Ethiopia, eastern Africa. (The earliest known fossilized human remains identified by scientists to be *Homo sapiens*. If the human remains found at Jebel Irhoud, Morocco, western Africa, were true *Homo sapiens*, then the early humans have emerged earlier than we thought and the originated ground of emergence will remain a mystery.) There are several things that we can reasonably predict their livelihood during that time. Their bodies were bare and without clothing mainly because they hadn't developed the knowledge to make clothing. Besides, they had no need for clothing because of the hot climate in southern Ethiopia (located in the equatorial area of the earth) with minimum seasonal changes. Their main food source was likely fruits, which might be plentiful in the tropical area. In other words, they were gatherers. Their bodies were likely small, which allowed them to climb more easily when collecting fruits from trees or to bend down to look for fruits on the ground. Since Africa is the most populated wildlife continent, they might also be hunters. They likely hunted small animals instead of big ones because they had only stone tools. Water and food were the two most important elements of survival for early humans. They likely stayed near the Omo River, so they had easy access to water. They couldn't go too far from their water source because they had

not yet developed water bags or containers. Therefore, their livelihood was searching and gathering by the river, where there was more
vegetation with more fruit trees. Living by the river, they might have
even learned how to catch fish for food. They lived in caves instead of
on the open ground to shelter themselves from predators and rain.
(There are heavy rainfalls in southern Ethiopia in the summer.)

As hunters and gatherers, they would continue to stay in one area
when there were still fruits to collect and small animals to hunt. As
the population grew, food might have become insufficient for a large
group, causing them to move to other areas to survive. Some of them
might have been driven out from their normal feeding ground.

Where would they migrate to? Early humans have migrated
from southern Ethiopia to different parts of Africa, except for
the Sahara Desert, which occupied most of northern Africa. They
couldn't go too far into the desert due to lack of water and food.
Many of them migrated to central Africa (now known as the
Congo) and the southern area of Africa (now known as South
Africa), where they stayed for more than one hundred thousand
years. They couldn't go anywhere else because the entire continent is surrounded by the Atlantic Ocean to the west, the Indian
Ocean to the east, and the Mediterranean Sea to the north. They
remained and became the ancestors of modern African people.

The majority of early humans migrated north along the Nile
River, which is the longest river in the world. The Nile River starts
in central Africa and flows northward into the Mediterranean
Sea. How did early humans find this migration route? The originated ground of early humans was in the Kibish Mountains in

the southwestern corner of Ethiopia. It is located about 250 miles (402 kilometers) east of the Nile. North and east of this area were the Ethiopia Highlands, an unfavorable area for early humans because of the rugged mountains and colder climate (most of the area is situated above five thousand feet) and heavy rains during the summer. West of Kibish was the plain area of Sudan. There were rivers and more vegetation, so it would be a more desirable area for early humans because of the hot climate, availability of food, and easy access to water. Since they lived by creeks and rivers, they might have followed the water downstream, searching for food, not knowing these small rivers took them to the tributaries of the Nile River. Eventually, they reached the Nile River.

The Nile River is the center of civilization in Africa. It is now, and it was in the past. Early humans might have settled and grew bigger groups by the Nile River. Along the riverbanks, there was more vegetation and a variety of fruits, and it was easy to find shelter among the trees or in caves. Life in the water of the Nile River was abundant. Frogs, catfish, crayfish, and soft-shell turtles could be caught with primitive tools. Therefore, the Nile provided prolific food, water, and shelter, which were the three most important things for early humans. Most of them stayed on the east side of the Nile River, since they came from the east. Few of them could go across the big Nile. They likely did not go too far from the riverbanks because vegetation became scarce away from the river. Outside the narrow vegetation area along the river, there were deserts on both sides. Therefore, their habitat and migration route were restricted to the riverbanks of the Nile.

Living by the water, many of them might have learned how to swim or got a free ride by floating down the river with dead tree trunks or logs. Some of them might have followed the Nile River and migrated farther north (the Nile flows northward), across today's Sudan, then into Egypt, finally reaching the Nile Delta in the Mediterranean Sea. This was not a short journey. It was about three thousand miles long (forty-eight hundred kilometers). After arriving at the Nile Delta in northern Egypt, they couldn't go any farther because of the Mediterranean Sea. Some of them continued their migration westward along the coastal area of northern Africa, south of the Mediterranean Sea. Along this route, they were able to find both fruits and seafood along the shore. They crossed today's Libya, Tunisia, and Algeria and reached as far west as Morocco, where their journey ended. (Archeologists have found early human remains in Sudan, Egypt, Libya, and Morocco date 50,000 to 190,000 years ago.) They couldn't go farther west because of the Atlantic Ocean. Note: recent discovery of early human remains in Morocco, which date to 300,000 years old, suggests either a new location of emergence or the migration from Ethiopia took place much earlier than we knew.

About 125,000 years ago, a group of early humans might have migrated eastward, crossed over into the Arabian Peninsula (based on archaeological findings and dating). In other words, it took seventy thousand years for early humans to migrate from their originated ground in Ethiopia to the northeastern corner of Africa. Why did it take such a long time? Of course, it is obvious that they didn't have modern transportation and roads as we have today. The main reason was that there was no need for them to move to another area. The Nile River provided them with prolific food and water and became the lifeline of early humans in Africa.

After early humans migrated to the Arabian Peninsula 125,000 years ago, they likely did not move directly eastward across the desert in Saudi Arabia because of a lack of water and food. They chose the coastal area on the south side of the Arabian Peninsula and moved north along the west side of the Persian Gulf. They followed the shoreline because of the availability of seafood. (Archeologists have found human remains in Israel, Oman, and the United Arab Emirates dating to one hundred thousand years ago and older.) When they reached the Persian Gulf, they might have been exhausted from their long journey and decided to settle without going farther east. Their population did not grow much because of the desert environment and its lack of vegetation and little rainfall.

About seventy thousand years ago, more early humans from Africa arrived in the Persian Gulf. As the population increased, there was a need to migrate farther for food. Where would they go? Early human beings did not have the knowledge of geography. They migrated to places wherever they could find food and fresh water. When there were no rivers to follow, they relied on the sun. The sun always rose in the east and set in the west. Besides, sun gave them light and heat. Without the sun, it would be dark and cold. They likely believed that the sun would guide them to food and water. This might be the first spiritual belief of early human beings. Every morning, they walked toward the direction where the sun rose. Consequently, east became the direction of their migration. (Note: this theory is my speculation, which explains why early human beings continued their eastward migration until they reached Asia.) They continued their journey eastward, across Iraq, Iran, Afghanistan, and Pakistan and into the northern area of India. When they reached the Himalayas, the world's biggest and highest mountain range, they couldn't cross over them. They had two choices to continue their journey. One was to go south to the hot Indian Peninsula. They likely did not choose this route because it was against their spiritual belief of going east toward the morning sun. The second choice was to continue their journey eastward along some rivers in the southern plain of the Himalaya Mountains.

They did not know that the river they followed was the Ganges River, the largest and longest river in India and the most sacred river in India for thousands of years. It might have also served as a lifeline and guidance for early humans during their migration. It flowed in a southeasterly direction across northern India for about one thousand and five hundred miles (two thousand and four hundred kilometers). The sun rose above the river every morning, which was exactly what the early humans wanted to see. They thought they were going east because they were following the morning sun. Actually, they were walking in a southeasterly direction because the sun rises in the southeast in the northern hemisphere half the year. The Ganges led the early humans to a doorway that opened into Southeast Asia. From there, one group went to New Guinea and Australia, where their numbers did not grow much. The other group went north into China, where they grew into a large population. Asia and Southeast Asia are the most fruitful areas of the world. The climate was warm and hot, and the entire area was covered with large and small rivers. Rainfalls were frequent throughout the year, providing plenty of food and water for early human beings. In this continent, early humans settled and multiplied. They became the ancestors of the Asian people. (There is abundant evidence of early human beings presented in different countries in Asia that date forty thousand to seventy thousand years ago.)

During the glacial period, the sea level was much lower than now due to most of the precipitation forming snow and ice and accumulating on the continent mass and poles. (Note: we are now living in a warm period after the last glacial period, which ended ten thousand years ago.) As the sea level dropped, many shallow areas in Southeast Asia surfaced above, connecting islands in the South China Sea, Indonesia, New Guinea, and Australia. The Asian continent thus became much larger. Early humans could move freely from one place to another, which were not separated by the sea then. They might have also walked over to New Guinea and Australia as early as fifty thousand years ago. When the sea level rose again and separated New Guinea and Australia from Asia, early settlers couldn't return to Asia. They remained and became the ancestors of the Australian natives. (Anthropologists classified them as the Aborigines.)

A common question is why did early humans migrate east to Asia instead of going north into Europe seventy thousand years ago? Europe was right at their doorstep. It was most likely that Europe was too cold for early humans who came from a hot climate. They probably did not have any clothing for cold weather. They had never seen snow before. They would not know how to survive in a cold climate. That was why they did not migrate north into Europe. Besides, they might have already had their spiritual belief of going east to follow the rising sun.

It wasn't until forty-five thousand years ago that a group of early humans left Africa and started their migration to the continent of Europe. By then, they might have developed the knowledge of using animal furs for clothing to protect against the cold climate. Europe is surrounded by ocean on three sides, plus the Caspian and Black seas in the inland. These waterways provided them with plenty of food from the sea. It was also a good place for hunting, which provided meat for food and fur for clothing. So, they stayed, and the population multiplied. They became the ancestors of the European people.

During the peak of the last glacial period (twenty-two thousand years ago), Europe became extremely cold, much colder than before. Northern Europe was totally covered by glaciers. This drastic change of climate triggered another human migration. Many Europeans started to migrate south to the Mediterranean region where the climate was slightly warmer. Some settled on the eastern side of the Mediterranean Sea; others migrated back to Africa and settled on the northern coast of Africa, south of the Mediterranean Sea. A large group migrated to the Middle East and to the Indian Peninsula (described in chapter 3). In both areas, European migrants found their new settlements, and their populations multiplied. They became the ancestors of Middle Eastern and Indian people.

At about the same time, northern Asia also became too cold for habitation. It forced people to look for new livable areas. A new migration also occurred among northern Asian people. Some of them migrated to North America using the Bering Land Bridge that connected Siberia (in the northeastern corner of Asia) to Alaska of North America. It is believed that the Bering Strait emerged as a land bridge between the two continents during the last glacial period (ten thousand years ago) because of the lower sea level. (See chapter 5 for more details.) From there on, they migrated in groups or tribes to different areas of North America. Some continued their migration into South America through Central America. In these two continents, they settled and grew, and they became the ancestors of the Native Americans. (Note:

The journey of early humans and stories presented in this chapter are my hypotheses. They are based on the information of archaeological findings and dating published in Wikipedia and other Internet sources.)

Archaeological discoveries in different countries and dating of human remains have established several migrations of early humans to different continents in the world. (Note: Different scientists may have different interpretations of migration time and routes. So far, they support that we came originally from Africa.) As early humans settled in their new areas, they were affected by the climate they lived in. In each region, they gradually changed their bodies to adapt to their new environments. Because of geographic separation that prohibited people from moving freely in the early days, people who lived in the same region tended to develop similar facial and body characteristics that distinguished them from people of other regions. This is why people in the same continent look alike but different from people of other continents. We also look different from early humans from Ethiopia.

CHAPTER 5

MIGRATION OF NATIVE AMERICANS FROM ASIA

ORIGIN OF NATIVE AMERICANS: Most archaeological findings of early inhabitants (Native Americans) in North America date to ten thousand years ago and after. Scientists long believed that Native Americans came from Asia because of their facial similarity to Asian people. This theory has now been confirmed by genetic and DNA studies. There are many theories and debates about the origin of Native Americans and the time of migration from Asia. Genetic study is complicated by the possible mixed descent of indigenous people with European and African immigrants, which might have led to hypotheses of different migration waves in different times and the theory of Eurasian origins. An early study (published in *Nature*) suggested they migrated from Asia in three waves. The largest migration occurred fifteen thousand years ago during the Ice Age. Most Native American populations were descended from this migration. Two smaller migrations also took place after the Ice Age. A more recent study of the genetic history of Native Americans concluded that Native American ancestors came in one single migration from Siberia (Maanasa Raghavan et al., *Science* 349, no. 6250). There is no evidence of multiple migration waves. The time of migration was no earlier than twenty-three thousand years ago. Thirteen thousand years ago, Native Americans started to separate into two groups of populations with different civilizations and cultures—namely, the Native American people in North America and the Native American people in Central and South America. (Note: the preceding data are collected from different Internet sources.) Despite the differences in interpretation among scientists, they all agree that Native Americans came from Asia. Exactly how did Asian people migrate from Asia to North America?

THE LONG-STANDING THEORY OF MIGRATION THRO-UGH THE BERING LAND BRIDGE: If you look at a world map, then you can easily see there is a narrow strait, the Bering Strait, separating the continents of Asia and North America. According to published data, the Bering Strait is fifty-three miles (eighty-five kilometers) wide and one hundred and eighty feet (fifty-five meters) deep. During the Ice Age, this strait was a land bridge between Asia and North America because of the lower sea level due to a large accumulation of snow and ice on the continents. Most precipitation did not return to the ocean, causing a drop in sea level. Even without the lowering of the sea level, the Bering Strait was likely an ice bridge between the two continents during the Ice Age because the water in the strait would be totally frozen as in today's Arctic Ocean. Thus, Asia and North America were connected during the Ice Age. Early humans could walk from Asia to North America using the Bering Land Bridge. This idea led to the hypothesis of migration using the Bering Land Bridge.

Let's think about the other options of migration from Asia to North America for early humans. Air or sea? You can definitely strike off the flight route because early humans couldn't build airplanes or air balloons. How about by boat? Early humans could not build boats large enough to sail across the Pacific Ocean without metal and modern equipment. Therefore, sailing across the Pacific Ocean was not likely either. As a result, this hypothesis was also abandoned. Although some scientists suggest that Asian people might have come by boat after the Ice Age when the Bering Land Bridge was submerged due to the rising sea level, they have not explained how they sailed across the Pacific Ocean without navigation instruments. Perhaps they meant that early humans used boats to cross the Bering Strait, not the Pacific Ocean.

Thus, migration on land was the only choice left. The Bering Land Bridge connecting Asia with North America during the Ice Age is a perfect fit for the land migration theory. In other words, Asian people could walk over to North America using this land bridge. It is also the only theory that scientists can choose. Subsequent studies tend to lean toward or add more support to this theory. They make this theory indisputable. Consequently, the migration of Asian people to North America using the Bering Land Bridge became a long-standing theory. Is this theory truly correct, or is there simply no other choice?

PITFALLS OF THIS THEORY: The theory of migration on land from Asia to North America via the Bering Land Bridge may seem indisputable, but it does, in fact, have many pitfalls. If we think logically, then we will find this migration route is impractical and impossible. I believe that land migration via the Bering Land Bridge is the most difficult, unthinkable, and deadly route. It was almost impossible for early humans to succeed in their migration from Asia to North America via the Bering Land Bridge. I will summarize my analyses as follows:

Possible Time of Migration: Why did early humans in Asia start a migration? A great migration was usually triggered by a major change of environment; otherwise, people would have stayed in their normal habitat. The most likely change of environment was the climate. About twenty-two thousand years ago, the Ice Age reached its peak (Dunbar and Waage, *Historical Geology*). Ice sheets covered almost the entire northern Europe, Siberia, and northern America. In America, glaciers had spread as far south as Wisconsin and Kansas (in the central area of United States). The entire area was like today's Antarctica. It was during this time that European people began their migration from Europe to the Middle East and India. (See chapter 3 for more details.) At the same time, northern Asian people also decided to move to a warmer area, thus setting off a great migration. In other words, the migration was triggered by an extremely cold climate. (Note: my prediction of the migration time approximately coincides with the possible time of migration concluded by Raghavan, et al., *Science* 349, no. 6250.)

Location of Habitation before Migration: The people who had decided to migrate must have lived in colder areas of Asia. Most likely, they lived in the southern region of Siberia, near the border of Mongolia and northern China, and in the coastal area of eastern Siberia. (Note: early humans likely migrated northward from Southeast Asia along the eastern coastline.) They probably did not live in northern Siberia or close to the area of the Bering Land Bridge. Because early humans were hunters who relied on reindeer and other grazing animals for food, these animals were likely more common in southern Siberia where there was open tundra and grassland. Even though reindeer were cold-climate animals, they likely did not spread into northern Siberia and the Bering area where the ground was totally covered by snow and ice year-round. It would be hard for reindeer to find open grassland and tundra—their feeding ground. It is reasonable to predict that Asian migrants formerly lived in southern Siberia and in the coastal area in eastern Siberia before their migration. In other words, their habitation area was far away from the Bering Land Bridge.

Distance of Land Migration: From their original settlement in southern Siberia to the Bering Land Bridge was about two thousand miles (3,218 kilometers). After crossing the Bering Land Bridge, it was another two thousand miles to southern Alberta in Canada.

Impossible Journey: We have to remember that the Asian migration to North America occurred during the peak of the Ice Age. The temperature was likely similar to present-day Antarctica. In such harsh and cold conditions, it would be very difficult for humans to survive. Even penguins must crowd together to resist the cold wind without food. Imagine how difficult it would be for humans to walk in subzero temperatures, facing blizzards on snowy and icy ground. We often hear that people die in blizzards just a few miles from home. It was almost impossible for early humans to migrate on foot for two thousand miles to the Bering Land Bridge. In addition, there were women and children in the group. They would all die before they could reach the Bering area. Even if they made it to the Bering Land Bridge and crossed into North America, they still had another two thousand miles of more difficult journey to southern Alberta, Canada. They had to cross over the Rocky Mountains, the highest mountain range in North America, and face rough terrain, higher altitudes, and colder temperatures. If they weren't buried by avalanche, then they would die of exhaustion. Let's think logically. The reason that early Asians wanted to move to a warmer area was because the climate had changed to unbearable cold in their habitat area. Why would they migrate northward to the Bering Land Bridge in the Arctic Circle, a place that was colder than where they lived? Therefore, migration on land via the Bering Land Bridge may seem to be a perfect theory, but it is unreasonable and impractical.

What if the migration took place during the interglacial time (a warmer period that occurred sixty thousand years ago)? Then it would be possible for Asian people to migrate to North America on land. So far, there are no archaeological findings in North America to support such early migration. If Asians didn't migrate to North America on land using the Bering Land Bridge, then how did they come to North America?

PACIFIC CURRENT DRIFT THEORY: I have another theory and interpretation. I believe that Asian people migrated to North America by rafts. They arrived to the continent by destiny, not by intention. To understand my theory, I will begin the story at the time of migration. When the climate became colder in southern Siberia and the northeastern area of China, local inhabitants decided to move to a warmer area. It was a matter of survival.

It is reasonable to believe that early Asians did not know of the existence of the Bering Land Bridge or of the North America continent, and they likely had no intention of going there. All they wanted was to move to a warmer area. If they started their journey going north toward the direction of the Bering Land Bridge, then they would quickly find that blizzards got stronger, snow became deeper, and temperatures got colder instead of warmer. They would have known that they had gone the wrong way. They would quickly turn around and head in the opposite direction (south). As the southward direction brought them to warmer weather, they would continue their southward migration. When one group of people migrated successfully, others followed. Even though they might not have any geographic knowledge, they would have chosen the right direction just by using common sense, and this meant going south toward a warmer area. In other words, they were moving farther away from the Bering Land Bridge, not closer to it. This is a more logical interpretation of how early humans decided the direction of migration.

As they migrated southward, inland migrants would find settlement in the central and southern areas of China. Coastal migrants might have arrived at the islands of Japan. (Note: Japan might have been connected to eastern Siberia during the Ice Age because of the lower sea level.) They might have used rafts to move from one island to another. (Note: Early humans might have learned how to build rafts to cross rivers during their migration from southern China to northern China because there were several major rivers in China that early humans would not be able to cross without rafts. Otherwise, they would not have reached as far north as Siberia. In southern Asia, they likely used bamboo to build rafts, which have been used until modern day. In northern China, they likely used tree trunks.) As they migrated to the southern islands of Japan, they couldn't go any farther. The ocean trapped them on all sides.

As the climate continued getting colder, they knew they would die if they stayed. They had no choice but to continue their journey into the ocean by raft, hoping there were islands or land on the other side. They decided to build bigger rafts, using straps made from animal skins to tie the tree trunks together. They saved their game meat. A big game meat could provide food for a family for several months. Meat would not turn bad in subzero temperatures, as it would be frozen. They moved big ice blocks onto the rafts, which would give them fresh water during their voyage. They might even know how to use animal skins for sails and tree branches for paddles. Thus, they were ready to set sail into the big ocean. They might have left alone or in groups. Their original plan was to sail south toward a warmer climate.

As the rafts slowly left the island, they sailed southward into the ocean. Not too far from the island, they noticed their rafts drifting northeast. No matter how they tried to steer the rafts in a southerly direction, the rafts continued drifting northeast. This was because their rafts got caught in the Pacific Ocean's current, which flowed in a northeasterly direction along the east coast of Japan. There was not much they could do, and they did not know where they were going. Their lives depended on their fate. Fortunately, the Pacific current was warm, which kept them from freezing. They also had food and water that could last for several months. They let the current guide their fate.

The Pacific Ocean current is the largest oceanic current in the world. It flows clockwise in the northern hemisphere in a semicircle. It flows from the Philippine Islands north to Japan, from Japan northeast to the Bering Sea, and east toward North America. It turns south along the West Coast of America, flowing toward the equator. Any object caught in the current will be carried by it in a big clockwise movement. In March 2011, the Tohoku area of northeastern Japan was struck by a very powerful undersea earthquake, which created one of the largest tsunamis in the world. It destroyed coastal cities and washed away buildings. Debris and wreckage were swept into the sea and drifted across the ocean by the Pacific current. After about six months, tsunami debris arrived at the shores of western Canada and the United States. This gives you an idea of the speed of the Pacific current and the approximate time for an object to drift from Japan to the West Coast of North America. Although many debris didn't reach the shore until two years later, it was because they were swept into the central area of the Pacific where the current flow is slower and less consistent. We also have to remember that the modern-day Pacific current is relatively slow moving because it is slowed down by the southern flow of the cold current from the Arctic Ocean through the Bering Strait. It also loses speed south of the Bering Sea, where it splits into one easterly flow toward Canada and one into the Arctic Ocean.

During the Ice Age, the Pacific current might have been much faster moving than now because the Bering Strait emerged to become land, which blocked the cold current from the Arctic Ocean. The Pacific current did not have to flow against the Arctic current, and the entire warm current flowed eastward toward Canada at much higher speeds. In addition, if an object were floating above the water, such as a raft with a sail, then it would catch the wind to increase its speed and shorten its drifting time. In other words, Asian migrants might have reached the West Coast of North America from Japan in about three months or less.

After a month or two of drifting in the ocean, some rafts might have drifted ashore in the area now known as Anchorage, Alaska. Although Anchorage is situated far north near the Arctic Circle, the warm Pacific current made the area habitable for Asian migrants. Some of them settled and became the ancestors of northern Native Americans. Those people who had missed the landing in Alaska continued drifting. The current took them southward along the West Coast of North America. Some had drifted ashore in different coastal areas of Canada and the United States. There, Asian migrants settled and multiplied. When the Ice Age ended about ten thousand years ago, snow had started to melt on the Rocky Mountains, and the glaciers had retreated north from the Great Lakes area, leaving a vast open land in the interior of the continent. Early settlers started to venture east across the Rocky Mountains in groups. Each group became a tribe, occupying different places in the North American continent. They became the ancestors of North American native people. (Note: This is why many archeological finds in the interior of the continent date to ten thousand years ago and later. Asian migrants actually arrived at the West Coast much earlier but couldn't cross over the Rocky Mountains because the terrain was covered with thick snow and glaciers.)

Some Asian migrants drifted ashore in the coastal region of Mexico. It is not known whether they came with the original migration group and missed the opportunity of landing in Canada and the United States or whether they came separately at a different time. They also found a new settlement in Mexico. Later, they migrated south to Central and South America. They went as far south as the southern tip of Chile. They became the ancestors of the Central and South American native people. They developed advanced civilizations and knowledge of astronomy, geometry, and arithmetic. Some of the ancient structures they built several hundred years ago, such as the pyramids, monuments, temples, and cities, show advanced architecture and design. They were truly amazing. Some of their creations remain mysteries.

It is reasonable to conclude that Asian people arrived in America by destiny, not by intention. Their original destination was a warm place in southern Asia. They had no idea of the existence of the North American continent, and they did not know that the current in the Pacific Ocean would take them around the northern Pacific Rim and into North America. It was fate that took them to America.

As you can see, the Pacific current drift theory presents a much more reasonable migration route than land migration via the Bering Land Bridge. Early Asian people had a much better chance of reaching North America on rafts than on foot. It was a shorter distance, easier and faster and with fewer fatalities. The warm current provided a mild temperature of 32° Fahrenheit (0° C). They didn't have to do very much. They sat on their rafts and waited for fate to guide them to their destination. Conversely, land migration via the Bering Land Bridge covered a longer distance over rugged terrain that was physically exhausting and with much colder temperatures, deep snow and blizzards, and the risk of more fatalities. Under such harsh conditions, it was almost impossible for early humans to reach North America on land. If my interpretation is correct, then it overturns the long-standing theory of migration via the Bering Land Bridge.

FACIAL TRAITS OF NATIVE AMERICAN PEOPLE: The facial traits of Native American people are very similar to Asian people. However, they do look different from most Asian people. The most distinct trait that characterizes Native Americans is their eagle nose, which resembles the curved beak of an eagle. An eagle nose is uncommon among Asian people. Most Asian people have medium-size, neutral noses, which are not as high and narrow as the European people and not as low and wide as the African people. Why did Native American people have eagle noses?

The development of eagle noses among Native Americans is a mystery. Unlike the Middle Eastern people whose hooked noses were developed to prevent their facial scarves from sliding down (see section 3.3—HOOKED NOSES for more details), Native Americans did not use facial scarves. I have a hypothesis that may explain the origin of eagle noses among Native Americans. First, Native American people originally came from northern Asia, probably in southern Siberia. The climate was very cold there as in Europe. Most inhabitants developed high noses like Europeans due to blowing their noses frequently in the cold climate. (See section 2.1—NOSES for more details.) In other words, when Asian migrants arrived in North America, they already had high noses. Second, since early natives relied on hunting and fishing for food, the flying and fishing skills of the eagle amazed them. They likely worshiped the eagle (this was long before Europeans introduced modern religion to Native Americans) and wanted to look like it. They decorated their headwear and dress with eagle feathers, and they danced like an eagle. They wanted their noses curved like an eagle's beak. Those individuals who had eagle noses often became tribal leaders. Eagle noses came to symbolize a brave warrior. Naturally, most people wanted to have eagle noses. They started to push their nose bridges higher and pull their nose tips down and curved inward to make them look like eagle beaks. Since human noses are formed of soft cartilage and fleshy tissues, they can be altered over time. After many generations, many natives developed eagle noses, which eventually became a genetic trait among them.

This hypothesis may seem to be ridiculous. In reality, artificial alteration of the human body happened in the past just as it does in modern days. Different cultures have different perceptions of beauty. People have used different methods to achieve their perception of looks. In ancient China, people perceived women with small breasts as attractive. Parents would bind their daughters' breasts during puberty to prevent them from growing big. This traditional practice led to genetically smaller breasts among Chinese girls. In Thailand, some tribes considered long necks beautiful. They put brass rings around young girls' necks to push their heads up and their shoulders down. This forced the neck to grow longer. In Europe, women wore tight girdles to make their waists smaller, so they looked more beautiful and feminine. Similar practices are found in modern society and are even more dramatic. People use plastic surgery to change the look of their eyes, noses, lips, cheeks, and skin. Thus, what early Native Americans did to their noses is no different from what we do to our faces today.

Another facial characteristic worth mentioning is Native Americans' eyes, which are different from many Asian people. Since Native American people came from northern Asia, you may wonder why they didn't have slender eyes like Chinese, Korean, and Japanese people. This is because they left Asia about twenty-two thousand years ago during the Ice Age. The trait of slender eyes among the Chinese was developed after the Ice Age. (See section 2.3—EYE SIZE for more details.) In other words, Native American people left Asia before the development of slender eyes among northern Asians.

WHY ARE NATIVE AMERICAN PEOPLE CALLED AMERICAN INDIANS? When Christopher Columbus first landed in America (an island in the Caribbean Sea), he mistakenly believed that he had arrived at the Indian Ocean. (Europeans referred to all south and east Asia as India.) He called the native people he saw the "Indians." This mistake was soon recognized, but the name Indians remained for the indigenous people of America. To distinguish them from Indians of India, they were called American Indians. Acknowledgment: I initially learned this story from my son Simon Chiang and have confirmed it via Internet sources. (Note: many Asian people do not know this American history.)

Some people may think that the term American Indian is racist and have suggested the term Native American instead. The truth is that the majority of indigenous people of America have no objection to either term. They believe that both Native American and American Indian are acceptable, although some prefer to use their tribal names instead.

CHAPTER 6

MIGRATION OF CHINESE PEOPLE TO JAPAN

HISTORICAL STORY: The first emperor of China, Qin Shi Huang, defeated the other six Warring States and unified China for the first time in 221 BC. He was most famous for his construction of the Great Wall of China and his terracotta warriors and horses buried in his tomb. He was also well known for his obsession of seeking immortality. He wanted to find the elixir of life, which would help him live forever.

Xu Fu, a sorcerer in the emperor's court, told the emperor there was a thousand-year-old immortal living in the Penglai Mountains in the East Sea. Xu Fu was sent to find the elixir of life in 219 BC. His fleet included three thousand virgin girls and boys who would be used as gifts in exchange for the elixir of life. After several years of searching, Xu Fu returned without reaching the Penglai Mountains. He told the emperor that a giant sea monster blocked his fleet. He asked for an army of warriors and archers to kill the monster so that he could reach the island. The emperor was so obsessed with achieving immortality that he immediately granted Xu Fu's request. Xu Fu left on his second expedition armed with warriors and archers. He never returned. It was speculated that he didn't return because he was afraid that he would be executed for failing to find the elixir of life. It was believed that he had found an island (now known as Japan), settled, and started his own kingdom.

Meanwhile, the emperor became more obsessed with achieving immortality. He realized that Xu Fu probably had fled or been killed by the sea monster. He ordered a third expedition. This time, he held the family members of the fleet as hostages, stating that they would be executed if the expedition team did not return. At last, the good news had reached the capital that the expedition team had brought back the herb that would help the emperor live forever. As the sorcerer held the herb above his head and walked toward the emperor in the long palace corridor, a person ran out, grabbed the herb, and swallowed it whole. The emperor was so fiercely angry that he ordered the guard to execute the person immediately. The person cried loudly, "My king, I did it because of my loyalty to you. I wanted to test the herb before you eat it. If it is poison, then I wanted to die for you. If it is a true immortal herb, then they can find more." Since there were many assassination attempts to kill the emperor previously, the emperor believed that it was possible that someone might want to poison him. He pardoned the person to encourage more loyalty from his people.

In his desperate attempts to achieve immortality, the emperor also ordered court doctors and alchemists to refine potions and pills to help him live forever. Many of these potions and pills contained mercury. Instead of achieving immortality, the emperor died at the young age of forty-nine. It was believed he died of mercury poisoning. (Note: This story is well known in China. Many high school students have learned it in history class. However, different history teachers may have told the story differently. These stories are also described on the Internet.)

FROM CHINESE TO JAPANESE PEOPLE: I speculate that Xu Fu made up the story of a thousand-year-old immortal living on an island in the East Sea just to gain the emperor's favor. To his surprise, the emperor believed every word he said and immediately ordered Xu Fu to find the elixir of life. In his expedition, Xu Fu discovered the islands of Japan and saw the beautiful Mount Fuji, which he later described as the Penglai Mountains. He also found that there were indigenous people living on the islands and that the lands were fertile. Xu Fu planned to escape the emperor's control. He realized that it would be punishment by death if he didn't find the elixir of life. However, he didn't settle on the island during his first expedition because he didn't have an army to take control of the native people. He made up another story on his return to China, telling the emperor that a giant sea monster blocked his fleet and that he needed an army of warriors and archers to kill it. His story had again convinced the emperor, who was obsessed with immortality. Xu Fu's second expedition was even bigger than the first, accompanied by an army of warriors and archers, together with more people, rice seeds, medicine, and supplies because he had no plan of returning. When he arrived at the islands of Japan the second time, his army took control of the natives who were still hunters, fishers, and gatherers. He made himself the king of the island, which is now known as Japan.

It was said that Xu Fu's second expedition in 210 BC included several thousand men and women, together with an army of warriors. This group of Chinese people had settled on the islands of Japan and started a new life. Most important of all, their descendants and subsequent marriages with the indigenous people produced a new population and culture, now called the Japanese people.

As Xu Fu took control of the island, his group of Chinese people likely became the core group of his monarchy. Presumably, his descendants inherited the monarch for generations. Xu Fu also introduced knowledge of agriculture, medicine, and tools to the indigenous people on the island and changed their livelihoods. He introduced Chinese words and writing to Japan. Before the Chinese arrival, there were no writing systems or historical records in Japan. Chinese writing and language were used in the courts in the early days. It wasn't until the eighth century AD that a new writing system was created in combination with Chinese characters to simplify writing and to accommodate Japanese language.

For many generations, the early settlers did not return to China because they were afraid they would be executed if they were caught. It wasn't until the sixth century AD that some Chinese descendants were encouraged to go back to China for a visit. It was then that they learned the Qin Dynasty was short-lived. China had changed dynasties several times. They were no longer fugitives. Since then, people from Japan came to China frequently to learn Chinese culture, literature and writing, art and architecture, philosophy and Buddhism, and so on, which greatly influenced Japanese culture. During the same time, some Chinese traders might have also come to Japan and settled, increasing the migration of Chinese people to Japan.

SUMMARY: The existence of Xu Fu and his arrival with a large group of Chinese people in Japan is likely true. He existed in Chinese history as well as in Japanese history. A statue of Xu Fu is erected in Weihai, Shandong, China. Xu Fu is also worshipped in Japan as the god of agriculture and the god of medicine. There are several temples of Xu Fu in many places in Japan as well as a tomb in Shingu, Japan. (The preceding information is collected from Internet sources.) The time of Xu Fu's arrival coincided with several important changes in Japanese history—namely, the starting of rice cultivation in Japan, the end of the Jomon period (10,000 to 300 BC, the era of pottery), the beginning of the Yayoi period (rice farming began in 300 BC), and the formation of central government, writing, architecture, and social classes in Japan. If these historical stories are true, then Xu Fu might be the first emperor of Japan.

Japanese history states that the first emperor of Japan was Emperor Jimmu and that he was a direct descendant of the sun goddess. His reign dated from 660 to 585 BC. It is said that the royal family of modern Japan descended from Jimmu through an unbroken succession. In an article published by Yamatosaxon ("Was Japan's First Emperor a Chinese refugee?" in the *Daily Beagle*, thedailybeagle.net 2014/03/30), Yamatosaxon noted that most modern scholars doubt that Emperor Jimmu ever existed as well as the succeeding nine emperors of Japan. They consider that Emperor Jimmu was a mythical figure and legend because there are no written records or archeological supports. Yamatosaxon also cast the possibility that the first emperor of Japan might be Xu Fu. It is hard not to wonder that if Emperor Jimmu truly established Japanese monarchy three hundred years before Xu Fu, then why were there no major changes in Japan during Emperor Jimmu's reign? Why did most of the changes in early Japanese history happen after the arrival of Xu Fu? Whether Japanese monarchs were truly descendants of the sun goddess or descendants of a Chinese refugee remains a mystery. However, there is no doubt that some of the Japanese population today are either direct descendants of Chinese people or have some Chinese ancestry.

CHAPTER 7

REINDEER LED EARLY HUMANS TO EUROPE

REINDEER AND EARLY HUMANS IN EUROPE: Among all the groups of people in the world, early humans in Europe have had the biggest change in facial and body characteristics because of the extremely cold climate. They migrated from a very hot equatorial region in Africa to a very cold region in Europe south of the Arctic Circle. They walked the longest distance in latitude and met the biggest change of climate. The new land was bitterly cold and barren. Why did they stay in Europe? Why didn't they go back to Africa or migrate to a different place?

To understand this mystery, we must first understand why they left Africa. The most likely reason was a major climate change in Africa. It was the Ice Age forty-five thousand years ago. The thick accumulation of ice and snow on the continents drew water from the ocean and lowered the sea level, causing climate change worldwide. Africa might have suffered from severe drought and forest fires. The habitat of early humans in the Nile River area might have been destroyed as animals left and fruit trees died. Survival became difficult. People had trouble finding food. To survive, they had to move to another area. This might be the reason they left Africa and migrated north to Europe. They didn't migrate eastward because it was difficult to cross the Arabian Desert, which was likely worse than Africa.

As they migrated northward, the climate became colder, which made it difficult for them to continue their journey. Then they saw reindeer. They are large and grazing animals and are not dangerous like big cats or mountain lions. They could take a reindeer down with several men hunting together. Reindeer are big game with enough meat to provide food for a group of people for many days. Suddenly, they found what they were looking for—food. They used the reindeer's fur and skin for coats to help them stay warm. (Note: reindeer have unique fur that provides excellent insulation against cold temperatures.) Unconsciously, they had followed the reindeer herd all the way into northern Europe. Reindeer are cold-climate animals. They became more common and more widespread in northern Europe. It was easy to find reindeer to hunt, so they had no problem providing food for their families in this barren land. Even though it was bitterly cold, they could survive when there was food, and they could stay inside their caves to avoid the cold weather outside. This was the reason that early humans stayed in Europe. You may say that it was the reindeer that led early humans to Europe. More importantly, reindeer meat contained high amounts of vitamin D, which helped early humans to protect against vitamin D deficiency in an environment of low level of sunlight exposure. (Their low level of sunlight exposure is attributed to prolonged living in dark caverns and wearing thick clothing year-round because of the cold climate.) Otherwise, they might have suffered from rickets, lowered immune systems, and cancers. Undoubtedly, reindeer were the lifeline for the inland inhabitants in Europe.

REINDEER AND SANTA CLAUS: When we talk about reindeer, we can't help but think about Christmas and Santa Claus. Christmas and Santa Claus began in Europe. They are part of European culture and have become a worldwide holiday celebration. Santa Claus is a Christmas character who is famous for his kindness and generosity due to the gifts he brings to children every Christmas Eve. You may wonder how the story of Santa Claus started. The name Santa Claus was derived from a real person named Saint Nicholas, a bishop who was born and lived in the third and fourth centuries in Turkey. There are many stories of Saint Nicholas regarding his joy of giving to and helping the poor. However, his portrait does not match the modern Santa Claus who is portly with a big belly. Saint Nicholas was thin, did not ride a sleigh pulled by reindeers, or laugh "ho, ho, ho." Even if he'd had a sleigh, it would have been pulled by horses instead of reindeer, as reindeer retreated to the Arctic Circle region after the Ice Age. Where did the story of Santa Claus and reindeer come from?

I have a different interpretation of the origin of Santa Claus. Although Santa Claus was derived from Saint Nicholas in the fourth century, the mythical figure has been deeply seated in Europeans' minds long before then. The historical origin may have started as far back as forty-five thousand years ago when early humans settled in Europe. When early humans followed the reindeer herd to northern Europe, they likely believed that someone in the far north had helped them to survive in the cold and snowy land. This man had raised reindeer and allowed them to hunt so that they would have meat for food and fur for coats. Otherwise, they would have been unable to survive in this barren land. They imagined this man as being old with white hair and a big beard, kind and well-fed with a big belly. He rode in a sleigh pulled by reindeer. They were particularly thankful to him for providing food for them during the coldest time of year (December). Their belief became a legendary story that was passed down from generation to generation.

It wasn't until the end of the Ice Age (about ten thousand years ago) that early humans in Europe started to practice agriculture and raise sheep for meat. They no longer relied on reindeer for food. At the same time, reindeer retreated farther north as the climate became warmer in Europe. However, people continued telling their children about this white-bearded old man from the North Pole who would bring them gifts in his sleigh pulled by reindeer one night in December. To dramatize the story, they would tell the kids that this old man often laughed "ho, ho, ho." Sometimes he used this as a voice signal to command the reindeer to start or slow the sleigh. However, they never knew the name of this old man. When Saint Nicholas's generosity and kindness proved similar to this old man, people started to call this mythical old man Santa Claus. Soon, Europeans started to portray Santa Claus as the traditional stories were told—an old, kind, portly man with white hair and a big beard sitting in a sleigh pulled by reindeer.

Although the preceding story is my own hypothesis, it just may be a part of the rich history of early Europeans that we don't know. If we didn't study the development of facial traits, then we would never know that reindeer led early humans into Europe. If we didn't know the story of the reindeer, then we would not be able to predict that the mythical figure of Santa Claus existed in European history long before Saint Nicholas.

Every facial trait tells a story of our ancestors.
Together, they form the history of early humans.

CHAPTER 8

WHAT WILL OUR FUTURE
GENERATIONS LOOK LIKE?

You have learned some of the history of early humans and how they have developed their genetic facial characteristics. Now, let's talk about the future. What will our future generations look like?

Today, the world population is represented by many different groups of people with different facial traits. However, this phenomenon will not last forever. The facial traits we have today are not the end of facial development. Our facial characteristics will continue to change over time, mainly because we are facing continuous environmental changes, such as climate, culture, globalization, modernization, and industrialization. More importantly, the increasing intermarriages of different groups of people will produce new facial characteristics like a big melting pot.

Climate does not affect human beings as it did in the early days. Air-conditioning and heating systems have improved our living environments. We neither have to live in cold and dark caves like the early Europeans nor do we have to tolerate hot temperatures like the early Africans. However, climate will continue to change in the future as it has in the past. There is no doubt that our future descendants will have to change their bodies to adapt to the new climates in which they live.

Globalization has made our world smaller. Modern transportation allows people travel more easily. In the past, it took years for early humans to migrate from one place to another. As a result, they were restricted to live in the same place or continent for thousands of years. Today, we are spread out in different continents of the world and move frequently. This will bring different groups of people to live together and commingle with one another in one place. Intermarriages will become common and customary. They will produce children with mixed facial characteristics. After many generations, perhaps thousands of years from now, most people will have multiple ancestries. The facial traits that once characterized a particular group of people will gradually fade away. People will have a new set of facial traits. It will be difficult to tell what original group of people they belong to. Based on the present-day environment and our everyday life, we can reasonably predict what our future generations will look like. Here are my predictions.

8.1—BROWN SKIN: Our future generations will likely have brown skin. This prediction is largely based on the melting pot theory that intermarriages of white-, brown-, and black-skinned people will likely produce brown-skinned descendants. In addition, light-skinned people will gradually increase production of eumelanin to protect themselves from UV radiation in an environment of global warming, which will lead to brown skin pigmentation. This type of genetic change in skin pigmentation is well documented in section 3.4—DARK SKIN PIGMENTATION, which describes how white European migrants changed to dark skin in India and the Middle East. Similarly, dark- or black-skinned people will also change to brown skin pigmentation. Because most people in this civilized world are well dressed, this greatly reduces the amount of sunlight reaching the skin directly. Their bodies will have less need for an abundance of eumelanin for protection against UV radiation. Unlike in the early days, human bodies were bare in Africa. They needed abundant black eumelanin to protect their bare skin from intense sunlight, leading to dark skin pigmentation. Today, very few people bare their bodies, even in the equatorial region, except during sunbathing. This trend will lead to a decrease of black eumelanin production among black people and change their black skin to brown. This change of skin pigmentations is not only possible but also well documented during the migration of African people to Europe and Asia. Thus, future generations will most likely have brown skin pigmentation with variable shades.

8.2—BLACK AND DARK-BROWN HAIR: As skin pigmentation changes, hair pigmentation will also change. Most people will have black hair. Some may still have dark-brown hair. However, light hair, such as blond and red hair, will be very rare. This is because most people of future generations will have higher amounts of eumelanin, which leads to brown skin pigmentation as well as darker hair color. In fact, the changing of hair color is occurring among European descendants nowadays. Many European children are born with light blond hair, which gradually change to darker hair as they grow older.

8.3—HIGH AND SLIGHTLY NARROW NOSES: Most people will have high and slightly narrow noses but not as high and narrow as today's Europeans. If the melting pot theory stands, then you would think that most people would have medium-size noses like today's Asian people. Why should they have medium high and narrow noses? Two reasons may contribute to this. First, future generations will likely face more allergies because of increasing industrialization, together with new products and materials coming to market. This will lead to more runny noses and sneezing. People will have to blow their noses frequently. When we constantly press the nose from both sides, this forces the nose bridge higher and narrower. (See 2.1—NOSES for more details.) Second, people will face more colds and flus in the future, which again will lead to more blowing noses. In early days, these sicknesses were localized. Today, colds and flus spread quickly around the world because of increasing traveling and the transportation of foods and fruits.

8.4—OVAL NOSTRILS: Global warming brings hotter temperatures around the world. Our bodies will need bigger nostrils to ventilate the hot body air. The trait of narrow nostrils that is characteristic of European people will gradually decrease and be replaced by oval nostrils to adapt to the hot climate. The big round nostrils characteristic of African people will also gradually change to an oval shape because of the increasing use of air-conditioning at home and in the workplace, which will help people to live in more comfortable environments. On the other hand, if global cooling takes place and our world returns to glaciation, then our future generations will develop narrow nostrils to adapt to the cold climate.

8.5—MEDIUM AND FLESHY LIPS: The thin lips of European people will decrease, as will the thick and full lips of African people. Mixed marriages between these two groups of people will produce medium-size lips. Their children will have medium and fleshy lips, like today's Indian people, because of global warming. Hot climates cause people to let their mouths hang slightly open and to leave their lips loose, which allows accumulation of fatty tissues in the lips.

8.6—BEAUTIFUL TEETH: Advanced dentistry and ortho-dontics, together with increasing knowledge of dental hygiene, will undoubtedly lead to more beautiful teeth in future generations.

8.7—DARK-BROWN EYES: Light-colored eyes, such as blue and green eyes, were originally developed to enhance people's vision in dark caves. (See section 2.4—EYE COLOR for more details.) They have become less necessary in modern days, since we are no longer living in dark environments. Our bodies will gradually change light-colored irises to dark brown to adapt to the bright sunlight environment. This process will also be accelerated through mixed marriages. When a person with light-colored eyes marries with a person with dark-brown eyes, their descendants will likely have brown eyes.

8.8—BIG EYES: The eyes of future generations will be big but slightly smaller than today's Europeans. The slender eyes of many northern Asian people will gradually change to a bigger size, since modern Asian people have abandoned the old traditional Chinese hairstyle, the main cause of slender eyes. (See section 2.3—EYE SIZE for more details.)

8.9—SHORT EYELASHES: I predict short eyelashes for future generations based on two reasons. First, the long eyelashes of European people were originally developed to provide shade for their light-colored eyes to reduce the glare of sunlight. Our future descendants are likely to have dark-brown eyes, which can help reduce bright sunlight like a pair of sunglasses, meaning they'll have less need for long eyelashes to provide shade for the eyes. Second, modern women use false eyelashes to make their eyes more attractive. This trend will become more common. When real eyelashes lose their purposes of protecting the eyes from dust and providing shade for the eyes, they will grow shorter and lose their density. This phenomenon is very similar to the cause of baldness among European people. They have developed genetic baldness because their hair lost its purpose of keeping the head warm due to wearing hats in the cold climate.

8.10—BLACK AND MEDIUM-SIZE EYEBROWS: The loose, thin eyebrows of northern Asian people will gradually increase their density as their eyes become bigger, as bigger eyes let more light into the eyes. Therefore, they will need heavier eyebrows to help reduce the sun's glare. On the other hand, the dark and thick eyebrows of Middle Eastern and Indian people will decrease their density, as people are now using sunglasses to reduce bright sunlight. Intermarriages among different groups of people will also produce medium-size eyebrows in future generations. The light-colored eyebrows characteristic of European people will change to darkcolored eyebrows as eumelanin increases among future generations.

8.11—SPARSE FACIAL AND BODY HAIR: Thick and dense facial hair, such as mustaches and beards, were originally grown to protect humans' faces in the early days. In northern Europe, it helped keep the face warm to prevent frostbite in extremely cold climates. In the Middle East, it helped protect the face from sunburn under intense sun as well as from blowing sand. Facial hair will gradually decrease, as we are no longer living in extremely cold climates nor do we have to stay outdoors under intense sunlight for a long time. In addition, we now have sunscreen to protect our skin from sunburn. It is reasonable to predict that future generations will have less facial hair (beards and mustaches). Thick and dense body hair served early humans in a similar fashion. We have less need for thick body hair for protection, and we do not need it to keep our bodies warm. Therefore, human beings will continue to shed more body hair as hair becomes less useful. Our future generations will likely have sparse body hair.

8.12—MORE BALDNESS: The gene of baldness was originally developed due to wearing hats in cold climates. People started to lose their hair because it lost its purpose of keeping the head warm. Today, the trend of wearing hats is increasing for many other reasons, such as sports protection, team sports, religious dressing, identity, fashion, and good looks. Modern women have increased their use of wigs, which may also cause hair loss just like men wearing hats. Genetic baldness will become more common among future generations.

8.13—OVAL-SHAPED FACES: Human face shapes were originally developed due to their sleeping positions. Sleeping sideways in cold climates caused the narrow- and long-shaped faces of European people, whereas sleeping face up in hot climates caused the round-shaped faces of Africans and Asians. (See section 2.11—FACE SHAPE for more details.) Modern living provides us with a comfortable sleeping environment. We don't have to sleep in a certain position. When one can sleep both sideways and facing up, it would produce oval-shaped faces. The narrow- and long-shaped faces of European people will decrease, as will the round- and square-shaped faces of Asians and Africans.

8.14—TALLER AND BIGGER BODY SIZE WITH MORE JOINT PROBLEMS: Most species in the wild have grown bigger over geologic time, which is well demonstrated in paleontological records. For example, horses were the size of sheep thirty million years ago. Human beings are no exception. We have grown taller and bigger than our ancestors. Our future descendants will be bigger than us. Unfortunately, they will also have more joint problems and arthritis. This is because we have cartilage at the end of each bone in the joint area. As the bone of the limb increases its length, it adds more torque on the joint. Along with the increase in body weight, it adds more pressure to the cartilage. As a result, cartilage in the joint area will suffer more wear and tear. Cartilage has a limited use, just like the tires of a car. After a certain number of miles of driving, tires will be worn down. Added to this is that modern young people are interested in strenuous exercises and extreme sports, which will cause more damage and shorten the life of the cartilage. Along with the increased human life expectancy, the cartilage of our future generations will likely be worn before they reach old age. This is why future generations will have more arthritis and joint problems.

8.15—BIGGER BUTTS: I predict that future generations will have bigger butts due to the fact that we are now sitting more than ever. We are spending more time watching television, sitting in front of the computer, at our desks, and in cars. While we are sitting, fatty tissues in the upper body gradually sink down to accumulate in the buttocks area by means of gravitation. This causes bigger and fattier butts. Another reason for this change is human adaptation to longer sitting times. Our bodies will accumulate more fat in the buttocks to make ourselves more comfortable so that we can sit for a longer time.

SUMMARY: These predictions regarding the facial and body characteristics for future generations are based on the present-day environment and speculated changes in the future. If global warming continues and accelerates, then the world will face major environmental changes. The sea level will rise, destroying most major cities in the coastal areas and submerging fertile agriculture lands. It will also change the distribution of land, sea, and vegetation. It will certainly affect human habitats. On the other hand, if the present global warming ends and the world returns to glaciation (as has happened four times in the last two million years), then future generations will develop different facial characteristics, such as narrower nostrils, lighter skin pigmentation, and thinner lips.

No matter what environmental changes the future holds, human beings will continue to evolve and to make ourselves better fit for our new environments. Unlike other living organisms, **we have the intelligence and ability to change environment, as well as the duty to preserve nature, making the world a more beautiful place for future generations and ourselves. We are highly adaptable. We will live on this earth for a long time, unless we destroy ourselves.**

EPILOGUE

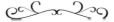

The term *race* and *race classifications* introduced several hundred years ago during colonial times has become a questionable concept. In the early days, European anthropologists and scientists did not have a complete understanding of the development of our facial and body characteristics. They thought that people looked different in different continents due to biological separation. Thus, they divided the people in the world into races based on facial traits and skin color.

Today, we have a greater understanding of facial traits. This book clearly explains and demonstrates the development of each human facial trait among different groups of people. They were developed entirely related to the climate and environment in which people lived. Early humans from eastern Africa migrated and settled in three large continents with totally different climates: Europe, Asia, and Africa. To survive, they changed their original genetic makeup to adapt to their new environments. Consequently, early humans developed different facial traits and body characteristics in different regions of the world. This is why European, Asian, and African people look so different from one another. Yet they all share the same African ancestry. Subsequent migrations have created a greater diversity of people in the world, such as Middle Eastern and Indian people, Native Americans, and Polynesians. It's the diversity of people with different histories, cultures, and heritages that make this world wonderful and amazing. Just like painting, you need different colors to paint a beautiful picture.

People's outer appearances may look different, but they do not have significant biological differences. In other words, there is no way to determine one's race by looking at his or her genes. Although some scientists claim there are biological bases for races because they can accurately identify a white European from a black African based on DNA, we should not quickly accept that as a scientific reason for races. Otherwise, we might as well say there are seven billion races in the world because everyone's DNA is different and unique. In each geographic region, people have developed their unique physical traits attributed to their regional environments, which led to differences in genetic makeup. However, this difference is relatively small as compared to the total genome. We, all people, still share 99.9 percent of the same DNA (Internet information). Therefore, the idea of biological separation among different groups of people is wrong. Race classification became obsolete without concrete support of biological evidence.

Furthermore, we are now living in a world of globalization. People travel more and move from one continent to another. It is certain that mixed marriages between people from different countries and continents will become universal. Their children will bear mixed facial characteristics. They will marry children of other mixed marriages. Their genes will be shuffled and reshuffled. Each generation will produce different and unique facial characteristics. If we have to divide people in the world based on different facial traits and classify them with new names of race, subrace, or sub-subrace, then it would be so confusing that no one would know what it means. Even a hundred names would not be enough to describe all the different groups of people with different traits. Race classification would not be applicable and would have no scientific meaning.

Since the use of race has become problematic in modern society, how should we describe different groups of people without using this term? It is best to use the geographic names for people who live in the same geographic area and share similar traits, such as European, Asian, and African. Nationalities may be used for more specific description, such as English, Chinese, Spanish, Russian, Arab, Indian, and so on; or in more descriptive ways, such as African American, Hawaiian of Japanese descent, descendant of French and Japanese, and so on; or by ethnic or tribal names. All these terms describe the person's origin, appearance, and possible ancestry without racial implications.

Thousands of years from now, it will be difficult to divide people into groups based on facial characteristics. The original traits that characterize different groups of people today will be melted down to produce universal human traits through mixed marriages and reproductions. Most people will have multiple ancestries. It will be difficult to tell to which original group of people they belong. People in the world will look alike. However, each person will have a unique look and identity, more handsome and beautiful.

No matter where you were born or
to which geographic group of people you belong,
we all came from the same ancestors
and share the same history of early human beings.
We are somehow all connected.

A LETTER TO READERS

Dear Readers,

Development of Facial Traits is based on my own observations of more than twenty years. The purpose of this book is to introduce my theories and interpretations to the public about how people have developed different facial traits from the same group of early humans. The main goal is connecting people in the world, wishing for better understanding and relationship among all of humanity. We all came from the same ancestors regardless our skin color, culture, and geographic location. Another goal is to inspire people to take an interest in our facial traits, hoping they will contribute their theories and information. The more we know about our ancestors and their lives, the better we can understand the origin of our genetic makeups and the history of early humans. By combining everyone's imaginations and creative thinking, we can restore the past to life. However, these goals will not be achieved without your help.

I believe that many of you have thought about the origin of facial traits but never had a chance to share your thoughts. I would like to encourage you to tell other readers about your opinions by writing a book review. You don't have to be a scientist to express your opinion. Who knows, your theory may be more acceptable and popular than mine. Sometimes, a controversial debate can help bring the truth to light. Even if you don't have a new theory, I still urge you to share what you think of this book and give it a rating. Perhaps you may prefer to tell your friends on Facebook and Twitter about facial characteristics. Each facial trait is a story of our ancestors.

This book helps us understand why early humans developed different facial traits in different regions of the world and how they survived in various harsh environments. Although our outer appearances are different today, we did not descend from different human stocks. We were all connected in the past. So, please tell your family, friends, coworkers, and book clubs about this book. If you are a teacher, then tell your students, and if you are a TV news anchor or an editor, then tell your viewers and readers. **You can help connect people in the world.**

Thank you for your support.

Sincerely,
Kam Chiang

ACKNOWLEDGMENTS

The scientific information, statistics, data, and facts in this book are mostly collected from Wikipedia, *National Geographic*, *Historical Geology* by Dunbar and Waage, and various Internet sources. Facial and physical traits are based on my own observations of more than twenty years.

The theories and interpretations in this book are my own creation and opinion. Other scientists' theories and interpretations are acknowledged following their descriptions. Knowledge of science is enormous in that it is impossible for anyone to know all the previous publications. It is possible that someone else has already written or published a similar theory or idea without my knowledge. Any similarities and resemblances are entirely coincidental and merely represent the fact that different people have produced similar interpretations about the same subject at different times. Originality shall go to the person who first published the theory.

I would like to thank my wife, Joan, for her review of this book. I thank my older son, Tony, who has a bachelor's degree in anthropology, for his review and suggestions. I also thank my younger son, Simon, who specialized in computer programming, for his review of this book and discussion.

I would like to express my deep gratitude to my university supervisor, Dr. Alfred Lenz of the University of Western Ontario, Canada, who gave me a research grant and teaching assistantship that made it possible for me to continue my graduate study in Canada. Without the knowledge that I have learned from paleontology and geology, it would have been difficult for me to come up with all the theories and interpretations in this book.

ABOUT THE AUTHOR

Kam Chiang was born in Wenzhou, a city located 230 miles south of Shanghai on the east coast of China. He lived in Hong Kong during his teens and in Taiwan in his early twenties while he was studying at National Taiwan University. He came to Canada in 1967, and he has been living in the United States since 1982.

He is a paleontologist and a petroleum exploration geologist. He received a master's degree in science from the University of Western Ontario, Canada. From his research, he has published several articles in the *Journal of Paleontology*. He worked for different oil companies in Canada during his early career and later as an independent geological consultant in the United States. He has made numerous oil and gas discoveries in both countries. One of his biggest achievements was the delineation of the Hoadley giant gas field, which was published in the *American Association of Petroleum Geologists Memoir 38* and in the *Treatise of Petroleum Geology—Atlas of Oil and Gas Fields*.

In 2010, he published a weight-loss and fitness book, *Chinese Secrets of Staying Thin and Fit*. This book was initiated by the fact that many people have struggled with their weight and fitness.

It presents new ideas and a fresh voice about weight and diet. It describes all the theories and factors that affect your weight besides overeating. It teaches you how to lose weight without extreme dieting and how to stay fit without strenuous exercise. It is entirely different from the traditional methods of losing weight.

He also published a fitness book, *Chiang's Exercise*, in 2014. Everyone knows that we need exercise to stay healthy and fit. Unfortunately, not everyone has time to exercise every day. This book was published to help people stay fit with just five minutes of exercise a day. It is his personal exercise that he has developed and practiced daily for more than thirty years. It is an easy exercise program without the need for equipment or supplements. It has helped him stay healthy and fit throughout his life. It will help you too.

OTHER BOOKS BY KAM CHIANG

CHIANG'S EXERCISE

CHIANG'S EXERCISE is a unique and unprecedented full-body fitness program. What makes it unique is that it can help you stay fit in just five minutes a day. It helps you build muscle, reduce body fat, and strengthen joints to reduce your risk of developing arthritis. It also teaches you how to do deep breathing to prevent headaches. It is suitable for men and women of all ages. There is no need for equipment or supplements. It is a complete workout with health benefits that no other fitness program can provide in five minutes.

MAKE IT YOUR PERSONAL HOME EXERCISE:
STAY HEALTHY AND FIT IN JUST FIVE MINUTES A DAY.
Note: *Chiang's Exercise* was initially published in *Chinese Secrets of Staying Thin and Fit*. This book contains much more information than was previously written.

Available from Amazon.com and other retailers.
E-book is available on Kindle.
Visit www.ChiangsExercise.com.

OTHER BOOKS BY KAM CHIANG

CHINESE SECRETS OF STAYING THIN AND FIT

This book helps you lose weight and stay fit permanently and effortlessly. It introduces a new concept of "Diet Without Dieting" to help you maintain a normal body weight without eating less or avoiding any particular type of food. This book also describes fifteen theories and factors that may affect your weight besides overeating, so you can take control of your weight internally and externally. In this book, there are no extreme diets, no calorie counting, and no diet pills or prepared-food packages. It also teaches you how to stay fit without strenuous, time-consuming workouts.

You will also learn
how to relieve heartburn without antacid pills and
how to do brain exercises for Alzheimer's prevention.
Also included is a new weight chart that shows the normal body
weight for your age.

Available from Amazon.com and other retailers.
E-book is available on Kindle.
Visit www.ChineseThinAndFit.com.

Made in the USA
San Bernardino, CA
11 August 2017